GREY CANVAS

grey
canvas

W. S. Lim
(Sok)

. . . .
four dots press
Canada

Lim, Won Seok (Sok)
Grey Canvas/by Won Seok Lim (Sok)

ISBN-13: 978-0-9849109-1-5
ISBN-10: 0984910913
LCCN 2011915324

Published by four dots press, Canada   www.fourdotspress.com

This is an autobiography by Won Seok Lim (Sok). Everything in this book is his
personal truth.

Most of the paintings by Won Seok Lim have been exhibited in the Winsor Gallery,
Phthalo Gallery and Artbeatus Gallery, Vancouver, Canada.

Cover and text design: Stephen Tiano Book Design, Calverton, New York
Editor: L. Stothers, Ph.D.
Cover photo: Won Seok Lim
All images photographed and painted by Won Seok Lim

Printed and bound in the United States of America, 2011

four dots press
Canada
www.fourdotspress.com

To Henkell Trocken

But the beast was captured, and with him the false prophet who had performed the miraculous signs on his behalf. With these signs he had deluded those who had received the mark of the beast and worshiped his image. The two of them were thrown alive into the fiery lake of burning sulfur.

REVELATION 19:20

The beast is the system, birthed from a collective fear of the *unknown* and over the centuries grown into a monster. Through our chronic avoidance of death, we have veered away from *trust*. The system consists of everyone, is structured by our markets and laws, enforced by our military and police, nourished by our media and upheld by us, its citizens. We all have *received the mark of the beast* since we've never been able to say no to becoming automatic citizens of our countries' micro-systems. We are born slaves with the drive to free ourselves. But instead of bravely facing the threat of annihilation looming in front of us, and thereby freeing ourselves from *the beast*'s consensual, fear-based delusion, we all continue to *worship its image* of a promised tomorrow. We do not see that our impatience with the present and love of tomorrow is what empowers *the beast* to continue to thrive in our collective consciousness. With its insatiable appetite, it has consumed everything and is still busy feasting on the last seeds of the planet. The only thing that can follow such long term debauchery is great economic and psychological depression, as *the beast* with its seven billion cells inhabiting nations all over the world suffers agonizing withdrawal from its own hallucinatory drug with nothing left to feed on. To overcome death requires death. As *the beast* falls, everyone dies within. No more tomorrow.

Time to begin living ...

PART 1

This is the autobiography of a guy who believed he'd emerge as the messiah at the world's end while his dominant life urge was to be a mass murderer. His name's Sok.

First Canvas: **Grey Canvas**

Sok kept his belief a secret from everyone. For most of his forty-five years, he struggled to uphold what he imagined to be the qualifications of the next messiah at the world's end. A few times he even felt the need to risk his life voluntarily. Although looking back he sees it was unnecessary, he asks himself now, *How could I have known that without trying?* He reflects that it must have been essential at the time, as he believes that in the end everything's inevitable.

For years Sok maintained a lifestyle of pain and misery because he doubted everyone. He accepted his difficult life while the rest of the world remained oblivious to the torments the next messiah was undergoing when he was hiding out depressed in his room. If people had known about him, they would've thought he was the most retarded person. They might've even told him, *Save your fucking self!* It's true that Sok needed more help than most, as without any friends he always only barely survived. From his point of view, however, having friends would've been unfair to his fellow humans since he would've had to keep his secret from them. That was why he had no real hope of finding friendship. He wondered when things would change but thought it would happen when he could explain who he really was. Then he'd be able to come out of the closet and be honest with everyone. *It's absolutely possible!* he convinced himself every day for many years, even though he wasn't able to walk on water. Given how brilliant he thought he was, some day he'd be able to express in words how it was that he was the messiah. People might finally get it, he reasoned, instead of deciding they didn't want to hang out with him because of his conviction, along with their definite impression that he really wasn't kidding.

In Sok's mind everyone else was crazy except him. That he'd already experienced the childhood state of still not believing anything particular about himself suggested that at least he'd known both states in order to qualify himself as a balanced judge of who was sane and who wasn't, while everyone else hadn't experienced the state of believing himself to be a messiah. This was apparent in the fact that no one else was currently making that claim. In Sok's unusual state of existence, he thought everyone else was crazy to call him crazy before actually experiencing what he was going through. Nevertheless, even though in Sok's view others were too crazy to become his friend, he still lived to see the day when he finally no longer had the burden of keeping his secret. He devoted himself to finding a way to prove himself and how he was going to save humanity. The truth was that Sok had never liked people enough to want to save them even if he could; on the other hand, the fact that he was so self-absorbed made him accept what playing his future role might entail.

After a lifelong dedication to playing his role secretly, about seven years ago, Sok had his first inkling of clarity. He experienced the phenomenon one day during his two-year voluntary lockup, one of several periods of solitary confinement he imposed on himself for the purpose of his own self-searching quests, an eccentric practice he'd picked up from his father. Since then he's worked to put the phenomenon into words. From his perspective he's finally found a way to live his role with no more secrets.

For Sok's journey to begin and come all the way to completion there had to be a cause, which he sees now as having been his choice. It was his first trauma that gave him a god complex, as some might call it, although he'd prefer to describe it as his choice to be chosen. Sok's initializing trauma happened after he was born in South Korea in 1966. Although when he was a baby he experienced the paradise of being well-nurtured by his mother, when he was four, his dad, after losing his job, dumped Sok, his sister and mom at his brother's place in a different province. His dad had never been nice to his mom, but this time he did about the worst possible thing. He landed his wife in a house full of about ten wealthy in-laws, including her mother-in-law and sisters-in-law. All of them were horrible to her because they felt that Sok, his mom and his sister were bumming off them, which they were. His dad had just sold their house, and without sharing any of the profits with his family he'd just stayed behind and used the money as he pleased, until it all ran out. Sok's never met a person as selfish and tyrannical as his dad.

One day during that time, out of the clear blue Sok's mom tried to suffocate him with his futon after she announced that she was going to kill him. He now sees she must have done it out of reaction to the harassment she'd been receiving from her husband and in-laws. She must've needed to feel the satisfaction of exerting her dominance over someone less powerful. He speculates that she could've chosen to confront her in-laws about their cruelty or leave her husband, find a job and get a place. But back then it was unheard of for a lady to do such things, though both Sok and his sister always wished she had. Nevertheless, being Korean, a woman and someone without any education or particularly exceptional abilities, Sok's mom must've felt the urge to take out her frustration on her son. Considering her suddenly acquired low status with her in-laws, she probably viewed Sok as the only available non-protesting victim on whom to pass down her traumas. She was like a bullied kid who needs to take out his frustration on innocent animals by taunting them. It's true that the physical harassment of children is commonly accepted among parents and teachers in Korea, but in this particular case Sok was absolutely convinced she was going to kill him. She put all her angry, resentful weight into smothering him with his thick, heavy futon. Even though he fought to keep breathing with all his life force, he was losing fast to the panic of suffocation.

Later as an adult, Sok experienced a similar anxiety once when he lost his breath in the cave of a hot spring. This was due to the emotional scarring he'd suffered from having his life threatened as a kid. Ever since the suffocation incident, he's also had a recurring nightmare. In the dream it's night, and there are mountain-high waves of black water, like a tsunami. He finds himself standing in the middle of the ocean on a small plank. In front of him are numerous unreliable boards randomly strewn to form a precarious bridge. He looks at it, feeling he can't cross it safely when it's in such condition. Then he hears a voiceless voice saying, *Trust!* He proceeds and then wakes up. It's only been in the last few years that Sok's stopped having these dreams. He attributes this progress to the fact that all his life he's pushed himself to face his innermost fear by teaching himself to swim in the deep ocean, cave water or any other scary-looking unknown body of cold water. One time he even dislocated his ribs while surfing in an attempt to overcome his fear of suffocation by drowning. As a child his trauma-based fear of water was accentuated by his parents, who never once granted him his wish to take a summer family vacation with the excuse he'd drown because not only didn't he know how to swim, but also they lied to him that it had been predicted by a fortuneteller.

Sok's mom was born during the last leg of the Japanese colonization of Korea and was a little girl during the subsequent genocide of the Korean War that followed. As a result, the world was a place where something incredibly terrible could happen at any time. All her life she's continued to live in sickly fear, simply not knowing any reality without it. As a child she'd experienced living with the dread of being thrown alive into a well with a hundred other Koreans at any time, one of the military practices employed during the Korean War to save bullets. However, unlike Sok who'd undergone the real experience of suffocation, for her everything was virtual, as in fact, during the war she'd lived in the south where there weren't that many atrocities, and so had mostly only heard of such things. In truth she'd never experienced any real physical torture or near death. With the exaggeration of her childhood imagination, however, the pictures in her head created from hearing about such acts of cruelty probably seemed worse than anything she'd ever faced in reality. Having been completely scarred by the fear of every situation being potentially horrific, even now in her seventies she's programmed to do anything to avoid potential discomfort. Therefore, with the drive of a crazed person, her life objective has been to avoid experiencing actual physical violence based on what's never really happened to her. Since Sok's known his mom, she's entertained a lifelong attraction to virtual scariness coming from her imaginings of what might or could've happened. Sok remembers that the only movies she'd ever take him and his sister to when they were four and six years old were either ghost or horror flicks. Often afterwards she'd play *the ghost game*, which involved her dabbing her face with fake blood, and with a real knife, chasing Sok and his sister all over the house. Then she'd go into her famous act, known in the family circle as *the dead person coming back to life*, by rolling her eyes like a crazy person.

Sok's fundamental trauma is similar to his mother's in the sense that it hovers around death. However, unlike his mom, Sok's decision to recoil from human brutality and aggression has originated in real experience. Though growing up he often found his thoughts concerning death and dying unsettling, he viewed them as acceptable in that he knew he wasn't reacting out of imagination-based fear, which in his opinion is what fear is. Consequently, unlike his mom, Sok was capable of making detached decisions.

While Sok and a lot of Koreans share deeply rooted insecurities concerning their environment, which in his opinion derive from the ongoing Japanese and Chinese invasions of Korea that have occurred throughout history, Sok's shouldered an added issue of mistrust stemming from his suffocation episodes. It originates in the experience of the person he trusted most, his mother, turning into a murderer in the next second. If his mother could do such a thing, *What about other people?* he speculated, his thoughts drowning and submerging into an internal chant whenever he encountered another human being. Over the years he's acquired the intensity and sensitivity of a cat ready to pounce, watching other people and his environment with the suspicion that they can turn against him at any second. His whole life Sok's maintained this edginess towards everyone and everything.

According to the general precepts of Korean society, it was a given that when he grew up Sok would inevitably pass on his own traumas to the younger and weaker just as his mom had done to him, so that someday he'd blend into the Korean hierarchy. As in Sok's mom's case of being docile towards her husband and in-law abusers at the same time as she was taking her frustrations out on her young son, Koreans tend to be passive towards their aggressors while behaving aggressively towards those they perceive to be lower-ranking. This is why especially in recent history, Koreans haven't been proactive against invasions, preferring to dump their discontent at being victims onto their kids. Resembling defenseless children, Koreans would've preferred to live peacefully with Japan and China, like a clan of comradely brothers. Nevertheless, that's always been wishful thinking, pretty much their only thing along with abusing their children. Like many Koreans, Sok surely could've found deep satisfaction and even compassion in provoking other people under him by passing down his traumas. In fact, given the relative intensity of his original trauma, Sok often would've liked to kill someone, like a ball bouncing back.

The truth is that Sok's never been able to stomach any kind of abuse of the weak. Instead of going the bullying route, since he wasn't able to trust his mother or anyone else except his sister, he became self-oriented. In Sok's view, even though his sister, Sun, had grown up in the same environment, he observed she always seemed to maintain an enviable air of cool detachment. What this meant for Sok's own development was that he had to work hard to follow her lead. Furthermore, he noticed his mom and dad also revered Sun's unique quality. In Sok's case, having Sun as his role model and best friend allowed him to focus on something other than his own murderous inclinations.

For one thing, Sok felt he knew too little about death to take another person's life, not that his choice to abstain from killing totally derived from considering the inconvenience to his victim. Admittedly, it mostly emanated from his desire to give himself the fairest possible opportunity, since he always retained the uncertainty that his murderous act might negatively affect the karmic pattern of his next life. He'd heard from grown-ups this could happen and was to be avoided, just in case there was such a thing as being a consequence of a person's choice. Having already experienced life's harshness, the prospect of his next life being potentially worse was unthinkable. *I'll figure it out*, Sok convinced himself, with an arrogance that came from his pride in being able to self-contain his traumas by not reacting externally. He'd acquired this ability early on through having to accept his own death. Since the suffocation incident, he'd never been able to fathom anything worse, and as a result, had become incapable of accepting the impossible. Accordingly, anything had become possible, even being the next messiah. Not only that, but Sok grew into adulthood without ever succumbing to the fear of threats or mistreatment, since he couldn't imagine anything worse than the near-death by suffocation he'd already faced. Ever since he's never responded to punishment threats from parents, teachers or any other authority, just as he's never felt the need to lie to escape reprimand.

Sok believes his suffocation experience has given him a rare insight into the core of the human existential crisis, which he locates in the mystery of birth and death. From Sok's perspective, birth and death are the same. Birth is the transition from being a fetus living with a limitless supply of food in a soft warm watery womb environment, in complete connectedness to his mom, to being forced out of that safe setting into the *unknown* at the end of the birth canal. As the water drains out of the womb, like a fish out of water and under the threat of suffocation, he undergoes hours of pain going down the narrow tube of the birth canal towards a total *unknown*. It's every human being's first encounter with the possibility of personal annihilation, or death of self, that culminates in a sense of self as being separate from his mother. It signifies the end of the cozy feeling of paradise and the beginning of the journey into the *unknown*. Right after being born, the drastic change in environment gives the baby his first sense of what comes after the feeling of the *unknown*. Through the birthing process, he feels the sharp contrast to his previous feeling of being safe in the womb listening to his mother's heartbeat without any fear of annihilation. As the infant goes through the birth canal he wonders, *What's going on and what will happen to me?* This is the same anticipation of self-annihilation he'll return to when he dies and asks himself again, *What's going on and what will happen to me?*

After birth the baby experiences more traumas through having his umbilical cord cut, feeling cold in a harsh, frightening environment with a sharper sense of sound and touch, and not being able to breathe with the potential aggravation of circumcision. Sok speculates that his own birth experience must've been like the sensation of suffocation he experienced when he felt abandoned by his mom, whose trust he'd simply taken for granted. As his doctor spanked him, he cried out in surprise and agony while simultaneously feeling relieved from the pressure of suffocation as he took his first breath. Immediately afterwards he was overcome by the curiosity of wondering what would be next. Reunited with his mom, he found his new food line to be interesting and agreeable in taste and texture. He finally felt reassured that his mom was still his protector, who after all was there, but whom he now perceived to be inside out. After the terrible death trauma he experienced going through the birth canal and being deprived of oxygen, he returned to his feeling of trust and felt secure in knowing he really hadn't been abandoned by his mom to face the *unknown* all by himself.

When a person's born naturally, he feels the *unknown* ends in a regaining of trust as he completes the circle from fetus to baby. After experiencing the feeling of trust that comes after first facing the *unknown*, he's again ready to live with his original trusting nature. Invariably, however, his feeling of trust gets forgotten. This happens because human feelings are different from the memory-generating thinking process. Once the feeling fades it's hard to retrieve, like trying to remember a dream. Nevertheless, if human beings had the capacity to retain their memories of being a contented fetus floating around in a soft internal environment and then being born into an intensely vibrant external reality, they wouldn't know the fear of death and would be able to say, *As when I was a fetus being forced from the womb into the* **unknown***, which though I was being born felt like death, it follows that my next passage into the* **unknown** *of death at the end of my life will also be a birth into a different state of existence, just like when I went from being a fetus to being a baby.* Since death means re-entering the *unknown*, something every person's already experienced at birth, he simply trusts, since he has no doubt he'll land in an environment he couldn't have fathomed earlier. If a person were able to remember his birth experience, he'd have reason to be overwhelmingly excited about his coming death, like a kid before Christmas. Unfortunately, a human being doesn't retain any memory of being a fetus and successfully being born. This trauma-based human psychology can be brought to light in the contrasting temperaments mothers often observe in their unusually calm, contented Cesarean Section babies. Often having been airlifted out of the womb onto the breast without undergoing the usual angst and torture of the birth canal, Cesarean babies seem to accept the *unknown* more easily than most and so on the whole live happier, more relaxed, trusting lives. But Cesarean baby or not, to a certain extent, everyone forgets how to trust over time.

The first time either a child or adult experiences a crisis that unleashes the feeling of the *unknown* and triggers the question, *What's going to happen to me?* his heart rate goes up as if he's going through the death-like-experience of birthing into the *unknown*. Disremembering the rewarding feeling of regaining trust and accepting the *unknown* of his birth, he dreads the *unknown* more than anything because it draws him out of what he's come to acknowledge as his safe, womblike, comfortably familiar reality. As a consequence, throughout his life he's terrified about facing death and the *unknown*, living in misery within an external reality replete with so many possibilities of dying and ending up having to confront the *unknown* that he's constantly on the watch for the next potential life-threatening situation. He'll do anything to avoid the countless perils that lie ahead that might lead to the risk of death, though he's always unsuccessful because eventually death is inevitable. Human beings have forgotten how to trust, so much so that Sok ventures to define linear history as collective, untrustful living. Sok understands that lack of trust transforms the enlightening experience of the *unknown-trust cycle* into a fear of death state in which a person lives in limbo, since no one in the universe except himself can make him trust. Regaining lost paradise or trust is something everyone has to do for himself. But if he were naturally to allow the process of entering into the *unknown* to begin and end in trust, it would be love and the creation of his new reality.

The interesting thing about Sok is that unlike most people entrenched in the human condition of not being able to trust, as he was undergoing his suffocation experience, he was able to tap into the same feeling of the *unknown* he'd experienced at birth. The fact that he didn't actually die during suffocation after thinking he would allowed him to be able to go through the feeling of the *unknown* and the experience of regaining trust as one package. His body remembered the whole loop and came to know how to trust himself while mistrusting everyone else, starting with his mom. What the suffocation episode meant psychologically to Sok was that he was reawakened first to the bodily memory of his birth experience, *Shit I'm dying!* and then experienced the relief of coming out fine. There was one complication in that although his experience of almost dying was transformational, unlike his real birth when he experienced the wonder of metamorphosing from a fetus to baby, he didn't land in a different physical reality. Rather, he ended up in the same depressing circumstances he'd been in before the experience.

From then on he became obsessed with retrieving his birth memories in order to be able to live in complete trust with himself and everyone else. That was the paradise he ended up seeking the rest of his life: of going back to the feeling of complete trust he'd experienced being in the womb and then re-experiencing the original trust he'd had in his mother after his traumatic journey into the *unknown* pushing through the birth canal. But quickly he came to the realization that there's no such thing as retrieving the memory of being born; otherwise, everyone would remember the experience of being a fetus. So instead he set out to investigate the notion that facing the *unknown* is all about the preliminary stage of regaining trust. He thought that once he had proof of that he'd be able to clarify that death's an illusion, and that he'd live eternally without fear of having to go through one transition after another. He actually began to be excited about dying and set out to recreate the paradise he'd lost when his mom had tried to suffocate him.

Throughout his life Sok's continued to be obsessed with death, putting himself into a few near-death experiences out of total curiosity and fascination. One time he had a dream that for him explained death. In it he realized he was in a dream. He told himself he'd wake up and he did. That ungraspable transition from dream to reality was the gap he wanted to bridge with the questions: *How do I catch what's in between? Is that the **unknown**?* He thought that once he pinpointed the existence of the *unknown*, he could demonstrate how death as we imagine it was simply the state of being in the *unknown*. If that state existed, then death wasn't annihilation after all, and there'd simply be no such thing as death. With the impossible life goal of unravelling the *unknown*, he faced the continuous frustration of chasing a rainbow. Sok was living in the midst of an unresolvable dilemma. With the drive of a mass murderer, he was the most tormented individual facing a lifetime of homework. He received his homework assignment from his suffocation experience.

After the suffocation episode, having directly witnessed his mom's stress in her abusive situation with her husband and in-laws, Sok vowed to try to make her happy, not realizing this was not only impossible, but also that eventually there wouldn't be any tie left between the two of them anyway. Nevertheless, Sok tried for a long time; in fact, he worked at it most of his life, remaining in denial of the fact that he'd never be able to trust his mother. From his mom's perspective, however, he imagined it would have been equally difficult to be with Sok. He speculated that living with him must've been like coexisting with a mistrusting murderer-to-be. Since the suffocation Sok had become capable of physical abuse, and for Sok's mom, this virtual probability was far worse than any actual possibility. Whenever she interpreted something as the first sign of danger, the short circuit in her head would go off like a breaker, and she'd consider any discomfort to herself to be a conceivable threat. As a result, she mistrusted her son, who from his own perspective was starving for a bond of family trust with his mother.

Sok long held onto the misconception that his detachment from succumbing to his murderous streak was his choice, but now he knows it wasn't. It took him forty odd years to grasp that either becoming a saviour or a murderer, diametrically opposed opposites, like good or bad, was still a reaction. Eventually he made a choice to see that it hadn't ever been a choice. Now after decades of upholding his choice to hold his judgment, Sok knows he's succeeded in becoming a choice maker.

That it's been possible for Sok to dedicate his life to understanding who or what determines his choice comes from the inherent contrast in his original experience. Upon receiving the trauma of suffocation after having tasted paradise, he felt the responsibility of becoming a hell creator. The contradiction between the nurturing paradise given to him by his mom and the hell of being almost killed by her, along with other accumulating traumas, caused Sok to pursue paradise blindly back to its source, like a junkie withdrawing from the strongest drug. With his murderous drive, his life aim was to strive to get it back. In his attempt to retrieve the trust of his lost paradise, he's identified two factors that were ingrained as deeply as instinct: his top priority was that in order for him to recover his own happiness he had to please his mother; but to make her happy, he had to figure out what was causing all the shit to happen around him.

Sok's mom had enlisted him for the lifetime quality service that Korean parents expect and set up by abusing their own children, since he had the potential and willingness either to kill or sacrifice himself on her behalf. As for discovering the cause of his misfortunes, he developed a keen self-interest in observing his own reactions to his environment and the people around him. He became obsessed with watching and listening to himself to discern how he prompted shit. This propensity had the added benefit of causing him to lose momentum in his outward responses due to his own self-absorption. It's always been a challenge for Sok to react outwardly since he tends to disengage to watch himself out of intense curiosity. Unfortunately, by redirecting his rage towards comprehending how he created the predicaments he found himself in, he often became a dumping ground for other traumatized Koreans.

Sok's experience of inhabiting the interstices between paradise and hell entailed living in constant doubt as to which realm he was in, and whether it was positive or negative. Since he was continuously in a state of mistrust, he developed a doubting, questioning nature. With attitude written all over his face he was fundamentally unimpressed with the world around him. Instinctively, Korean adults and authorities could smell his rebelliousness a mile away. Like an untouchable, he became the object of adult physical and psychological cruelty from his parents, teachers and even strangers he encountered on the street. They'd pick on his long hair, clothing, ways of talking and walking, posture, opinions and excitement at any hint of pleasure, so much so that as he was growing up he became skeptical about the likelihood of rediscovering paradise. As he persisted in his dichotomous quest either to regain his mislaid trust or succumb to his hellish circumstances, he looked for increasingly innovative ways of recovering what he'd lost. Unfortunately, Korea's the worst country to explore creative outlets.

Sok's observed that under persistent goading, Korean children are quickly discouraged from exploring and expressing their own uniqueness. Moreover, as Sok was never offered rational explanations for the harassment he received, there wasn't any point in disputing. This has made things more difficult in that he's had to investigate possible arguments and try new things to figure out what his life's been all about. But as in Korean society anyone with seniority is always right and has the final word, Sok wasn't able to argue. He realized he was on his own to figure out his path without ever having the benefit of a fair debate. Meanwhile, Korean adults will do anything to preserve their conservative standpoint by remaining helpless children who've never had to figure out anything new or develop a line of reasoning that might inspire, convince or educate the next generation. The way they've chosen to remain pampered and globally inactive has been to become copycats, lifting western concepts or Japanese cultural phenomena to back their attitudes and lifestyles without ever needing to show appreciation for someone else's effort. *Why should they, since historically, they've had a chip on their shoulders, justifying themselves as victims of an endless onslaught from the outside world?* This is why at a young age, Korean children draw the conclusion that it isn't safe to do anything new or different, since generally, adult retaliation isn't predictable or rational. The only way for young people to appease adults is to comply and imitate. In Sok's case, he couldn't find any role model offering a version of paradise he was interested in copying and recreating.

All through his school years, Sok witnessed and underwent teacher abuse that by North American or European standards would've been viewed as criminal. It was mostly physical and sometimes sexual. Like sheriffs flaunting their badges and with an authority gained through seniority and college education, teachers enjoyed inflicting alarming cruelty and discouraged any kind of rebellion, all in the name of discipline and education. More than once a year, teachers received an envelope full of cash as a gesture of appreciation from the parents of each student in an average class of seventy for the respectable, morally sound education they were offering. But if their violence was ever questioned, it was met with the status quo, *You don't understand the Korean way,* since eventually Korean children become abusive adults themselves, no longer interested in revealing the outrages they tolerated when they were young, but rather choosing to reenact them. At great cost to himself, Sok's been able to maintain the integrity of disallowing himself to become a child-abusing Korean by remaining open and interested in exposing everything. To achieve this he's first had to be at the receiving end of numerous instances of abuse in order to be able to own this position. In light of this, as a teenager it wasn't so difficult for Sok to imagine himself as being the only sane person.

Regardless of his bottomless drive to interpret the dramas going on around him, Sok was never able to settle on becoming either a murderer and finding a home in a Korean prison or blindly believing his reality to be a state of bliss in disguise. Nevertheless, everyday Sok took on more traumas just by being himself: a lost, inquisitive, non-conforming, long-haired, acne-faced young person. Through this accumulation of traumas, he was building up his capacity to be a mass-murderer when he grew up. Ironically, during the process of holding in his traumas, he became a martyr, rather than a murderer, whose purpose was to please his mother and eventually everyone else. But as he gradually came to realize it was impossible and exhausting to make even a single person happy, he started craving recognition for his dedication to collective happiness. What he failed to comprehend was that dwelling within the contrast between paradise and hell was a design that prevented him from ever receiving the recognition he felt he deserved.

When Sok was six, one day his mother forced him to beg for mercy when he felt he hadn't done anything to provoke her. As even then he didn't see any reason to comply, she beat him for hours, stripped him naked and then proceeded to destroy his clothes and books. What she didn't know was that through her suffocation attempts, she'd already instilled in him an attraction to and capacity for life-threatening situations. Like a moth attracted to fire, Sok became even more interested in death. As death had already become the deepest, most irresistible mystery, it wasn't a huge stretch for him to choose to die, rather than beg for mercy. At this point, sensing she'd never be able to reap the satisfaction of Sok's submission by beating him, his mom changed her tactic. She wound an electric extension cord around her neck and started choking herself. With her talent for *rolling her eyes like a dead person coming to life* and the added special effect of her gradually reddening face, she played out the part of preferring to end her life, rather than continuing to live with such a terrible son. Like a cat, Sok watched and waited.

The result was that she must've found herself caught in the dilemma of realizing that in order not to reveal the fact that she was bluffing she would've had to kill herself, but if she did that, *what would be the point of bluffing?* Her only option was to drop her pretense and take a bite of the humiliation cookie at having lost the poker game with Sok. But if she revealed this secret, she'd be destined to lose any future games. In the middle of her internal struggle, Sok fainted from dehydration, hunger and fatigue, and she took this as her chance to withdraw conveniently from her agenda. She knew she'd lost but consoled herself in knowing Sok was the worst person because he hadn't let her have the satisfaction she felt she deserved for having brought him into the world. Of course as a Korean she felt justified in her conviction that his lack of submission was absurd and morally wrong, like a government illegalizing the raping of slaves by slave owners. To make matters worse for Sok, her underlying message was that Sok would never receive recognition from her or any other Koreans for the rebellion he was planning, the one he believed would ultimately bring about hers and everybody else's collective happiness. Ironically, out of his desire to appear deserving of recognition, Sok had made himself a victim. He'd become an unsolicited saviour whom no one appreciated.

While Sok was going through puberty, another life-changing incident occurred when his family was penniless, and he had no hope of being acknowledged. Except for his frequent escapes into his imagination, Sok's reality was fraught with repeated instances of starvation from his parent's abandonment, gas poisoning from the coal blocks they used for heating their cramped living places, being forced for years in school to shave his hair and wear a uniform, not being allowed to date, being forced to study till midnight every night, being grounded for no reason, having his dog taken away, being forced to act as if he was wealthy for the sake of his parents while he didn't have hardly anything to eat, being physically abused at home and in school, having to beat up his father to stop him from abusing his mother, putting up with his mom's neglect and his dad's long term steroid addiction, and feeling rejected from birth through watching western TV programs such as *Wonder Woman*, who he'd begun to notice wasn't dating any Koreans or anyone else who had even the slightest potential of being his sexual role model. Eventually, with his most recent disadvantage of having dropped out of high school to join a handful of official Korean adolescent losers, he spent his days in a tiny single room he, his sister and mother shared. His dad had put himself into solitary confinement in a different province, his sister, Sun, was attending university and trying to have a life of her own, and his mom had escaped to her wealthy sister's place in a different province where she was staying most of the time. While Sok knew his mom went there to find temporary relief from her own desperate situation, she acted as if she were staying away to make scrap money for the family by taking care of her sister's children with whom she felt more connected. Abandoned and left alone without any money, Sok'd occasionally steal milk delivered around the neighbourhood. His only amusement was a radio he listened to in his bed. Despite the austerity, he felt that as long as he was alone he was fine because he dreaded even more the periods when his mom would return. During those times she'd yell at him constantly, calling him a loser the entire period they hung out together in the tiny room, until one day she tried to hook him up with a factory job. At that point Sok'd had enough.

Sok's killer side was sprouting out of the martyrdom traits he'd been developing during adolescence. In his head he'd run through the list of people he wanted to murder. Although he was still in denial about his mother, he thought about murdering some teachers. As at heart he was a martyr, it occurred to him that killing himself might be the most effective way of getting back. *You'll be sorry when I'm gone!* he'd think. Sok's burgeoning suicide plan had the added benefit of allowing him to satisfy his curiosity about death and dying. But unless he tried it, he'd never get any answers; so when he was about nineteen, he went out and bought one hundred sleeping pills dispersed from several pharmacies. He remembers feeling relieved as soon as he had the pills in his pocket. When the time came, he had his first western style steak with a couple of cocktails in a fine restaurant. Prior to his decision to kill himself, he'd wanted to sell his kidney so that he'd have some money to enjoy a few things, but hadn't been able to arrange it in time. Since it was winter, the season in which Sok's always desperately felt the need to get warm, he checked into one of those heated private study reading rooms where Korean students are sent every night to stare at their textbooks until after midnight when they fall asleep over their desks. For less than a dollar he secured himself a section of desk with a partition. He'd reasoned that since it was considered acceptable for students to sleep there overnight, no one would notice he was dead till at least the next morning. He counted his pills a couple of times and then took all of them with a bottle of *soju* (traditional Korean hard liquor). A few days later he woke up in the hospital.

As he was swallowing handfuls of pills, Sok got to experience a moment of self-betrayal: he was killing himself to get to know what killing was. He wondered, *Who's the part of me executing the act of killing myself to satisfy the curiosity of the other part of me?* For Sok, no one's more interesting than himself because he's the only one he feels free to experiment with however he pleases. He would've liked to conduct an experiment of killing someone else, if he'd thought it would shed some light on the mystery of death. However, he resisted on the premise that it was easier to commit suicide.

After the incident, having already experienced killing himself and knowing it wouldn't be such a big deal to do it again somewhat freed him. When he'd tasted near death by suffocation as a kid it hadn't been voluntary, but this time it had. On the whole he felt emboldened by the incident, feeling he was on somewhat equal footing with god in that he was now in control of his own death. He also got to know that he'd never again betray himself in order to save his own ass. From then on, like a secret agent armed with a cyanide pill, Sok was able to detach himself from the misery of being a poverty-stricken high school dropout and lost teenager. Now instead of being dragged into everything against his will he felt in charge of choosing either to continue his life or end it whenever he pleased. Feeling empowered, Sok decided to go on with his life out of curiosity. With regards to his mom, he'd already let her know he wasn't bluffing.

Around the same time, another thing caught Sok's interest. At night he'd gaze out his Seoul window at the red neon crosses for churches and green neon crosses for hospitals that lined the Seoul streets like a psychedelic cemetery. Christianity was becoming the craze in Korea, and he decided he wanted to check it out just in case he was missing something. Eventually Sok enrolled in a theological seminary to find out more about it. Having so far not found any answers to his existential questions, he'd developed an interest in spirituality. Nevertheless, after spending quite a while in the Korean Christian community he realized religion was as empty as a false pregnancy. On the other hand, he understood that if Koreans had been able to settle for being the victims of invasions, colonization and wars without any need of explanation, the invisible Christian God handing out unreasonable punishments and his saviour son would definitely appeal to them, like charity coming from the royal family. It came clear to Sok that religion was another helpless child dependency his country was inevitably in the process of buying into, going hand in hand with their admiration of America as having been their saviour during the Korean War. At that point Sok knew he had to get out of the country as soon as possible to test out whether his troubles were due to being Korean or being human.

Sok realized that further pursuing English was his only possible escape route. After picking up the high school he'd missed and teaching himself English during his university years at the theological seminary, Sok eventually landed a job as an ESL teacher. There he met Bari. Originally a hippie from California, she and her family had moved to Canada to dodge her brothers' draft. At some point she'd come to Korea to work. After a couple of years of teaching ESL together, Sok and Bari moved to Canada, married and spent about ten years together, first in Nelson BC, and then in Vancouver.

When Sok first met Bari in his late twenties, he was intrigued by her socially unacceptable qualities according to Korean standards. She was seven years older than him and had a dysfunctional teenage son, who was living back in Canada with her extended family. Not quite five feet tall, she was obese but had a strikingly beautiful face. Sok felt compassion for Bari's conviction to go on everyday while being stared at by everyone. He remembers having a similar empathy when he was four.

One time a beggar woman came to where he, his sister and his mom were living with the in-laws. About thirty neighbours surrounded this woman who seemed to Sok to be in her early twenties. Everyone was happily harassing her while she was begging for rice. Nothing's as pleasurable for Koreans as having someone clearly lower in rank to bully. Unless beggars or cripples really begged as pathetically as they could, they simply wouldn't ever get any handouts. Wanting to gain popularity as the lowest ranking member among the in-laws, Sok's mom suggested the woman pee in front of everyone in order to earn a little food. As Sok observed the young woman squirming like a little kid while everyone around her was rejoicing, he had a surge of emotion. Seeing how vulnerable she was under the blinding sun, he perceived that he and she were connected through their mutual feelings of unworthiness and dependency, which for Sok had come from his suffocation trauma. Sok felt as trapped in his slavery to his parents and Korean society as she did with the common people on the street.

Sok, Bari and the beggar were the same in that they were unloved, he thought. Never having experienced love and trust with his mom, at the onset of their relationship Sok thought he might be able to find this with Bari. What he didn't realize was that she hadn't had the same depth of trauma as him, and therefore, didn't have the capacity to understand Sok's obsessiveness and drive. Gradually she came to view him as unstable, though he realized that most other people would've come to that conclusion a lot sooner. But for Sok, being seen in this light was equal to family mistrust, as he'd learned from living with his mom who'd never acknowledged him for his depth of experience, loyalty, dedication, intelligence, talent or sensitivity. Unfortunately, feeling he wasn't receiving from Bari the kind of unconditional love he was seeking, he began to feel as lonely in their relationship as she felt his lack of commitment. Nevertheless, their ten years of marriage wasn't without enjoyment, and for Sok, came as an educational experience of North American living flavoured with the milieu of the sixties with its songs, movies, ideologies, books and food. At least Sok had finally found some people who made a bit of sense.

Like an autistic child, while living in Canada Sok often put himself into humiliating and embarrassing situations as crash course experiments out of a desire to probe his concerns and observe westerner's reactions. He thought he had to give this new world a chance before making up his mind whether it was any different from the one he'd experienced back in Korea. Gradually he came to see that although people outside Korea seem more progressive, they still operate according to a familiar biased pattern of dependency and reaction. Sok gradually came to the realization that much of human behaviour is based on responses to traumatic incidents often brought on by national events such as natural disasters and wars. *But were such incidents merely accidental?* Sok wondered. Coincidence was something Sok wasn't going to accept until first he made sure it wasn't him, god, the universe or some other power that made shit happen. He also thought nobody else but him would have the necessary drive to persevere in finding the answers to such questions. Even in Canada that was Sok's obsession. He felt alone in his desire to gain clarity as to why he was on this planet and what had caused him to feel so utterly lost.

Even after having lived in Canada for several years, a general motive in Sok's decision-making was to save his sister back in Korea who was dying of breast cancer that had metastasized to her lungs. It'd been a difficult decision for Sok to move to Canada in the first place knowing his sister was losing him, the only person with whom she could really relate. After all, growing up they'd been each other's family. So when Sok came to Canada, he shouldered the old-fashioned burden of an immigrant man who occupies himself with finding some way to bring his family over to the new country. Ultimately what Sun wanted was for her younger brother to become successful in Canada so that she and her son, Sang, could be supported by him in Vancouver instead of living with her doctor husband, Young, in Korea. Out of Sok's desire to rescue his sister he became a recognition-seeking monster, desperately trying to find a grand solution to his own success under the pretext of helping her. At that time he was unaware of his self-contradictory tendency to take premature action before considering whether he was even capable of assisting another human being. It's precisely this kind of preconception that's led Sok into making unsound decisions from his swinging perspectives of underestimating and overestimating himself, and subconsciously creating opposite poles of attempting to acquire recognition. For instance, during Sun's cancer struggles Sok spent several years writing a few books that in his opinion would be popular, but that ended up having limited success, despite the fact he'd worked so hard on them. One of them, entitled *Forgiving Children*, was a story about him and his sister, their background of abuse, and how they'd taken on the burden of the next generation of Koreans. Sun liked it. She died after ten years of devastating struggle with cancer, and Sok lost the person he'd always desperately wanted to be recognized by. If there'd ever been a person he wished to save, it was his sister, the only one who'd never doubted his intentions.

Strangely when Sok lost his sister, the only person who'd ever acknowledged him for who he was and responded to his need for recognition, he experienced a sense of relief, rather than grief. For the first time, he caught a glimpse of his obsession to serve others for his own need. He saw how selfish he'd been, which he thought was fine in itself but mostly counterproductive. Something had to be done. There aren't many people as destructively masculine as Sok with his tendency to sever ties, whether it entails a sudden breakup or killing himself so as to be utterly unavailable. So in his late thirties he broke off his marriage and went into lockup by checking into a Vancouver apartment to withdraw from everything he'd ever known. It was his own self-constructed rehab. That was the only way he thought he'd ever get to know the real Sok, the one who drove himself with all his energy and need in constant conflict of interest with himself. This time he'd go all the way, even if it meant ending his life as a necessary final withdrawal from any lingering attachments.

During his lockup Sok decided to use his painting as the medium to withdraw from everything. By then his book publication attempts hadn't been as successful as he'd hoped, and he'd launched a painting career, selling his work through galleries. Isolating himself for two years he devoted himself to his artistic pursuits, numbering his days by calculating his remaining money for food and two extra months rent, enough time to induce complete starvation, which in his mind was the last withdrawal he was ever planning on going through. After getting close to two years into the lockup, one day it became clear that throughout his life he'd tried everything he could think of without ever having the satisfaction of being able to say, *This is it!* He'd simply never experienced a satisfying state of existence. He could've enjoyed being wealthy if that had ever been possible, but he'd always been distracted by his spiritual inclinations, which were so prevalent in his life that he'd never been able to ignore them. Yet whenever he'd pursued anything along these lines, he'd never come to any satisfying clarity either. There were times he'd wondered just how much longer he'd have to continue. But he'd already done the suicide thing. Eventually towards the end of his lockup he ran out of money and patience. He was done with waiting. Yet there was one more thing he'd never tried because he hadn't been ready, and that day had come.

Next is the visual version of what happened to Sok.

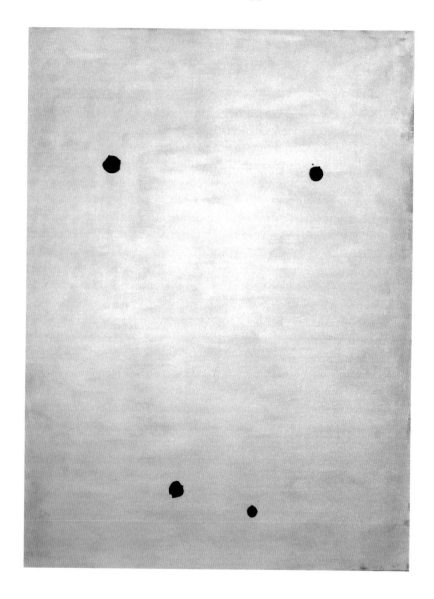

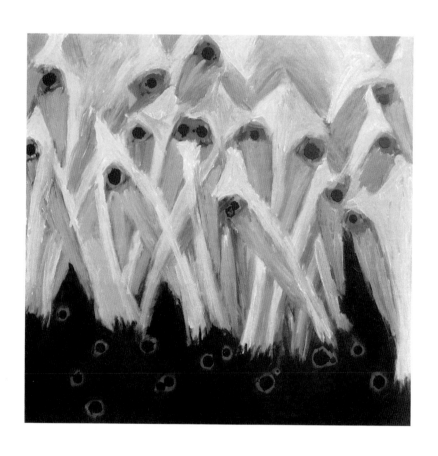

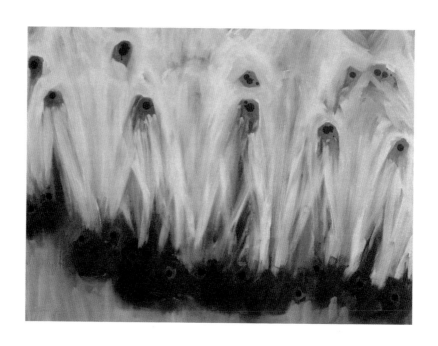

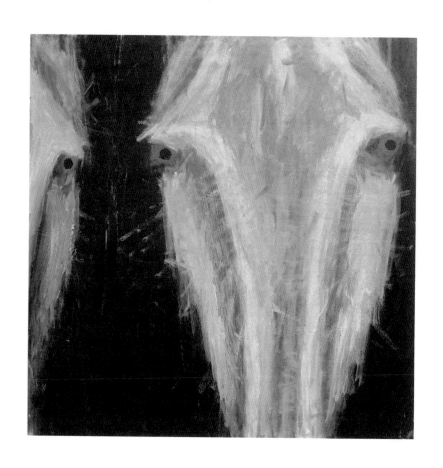

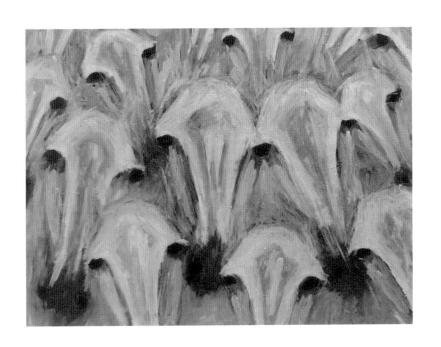

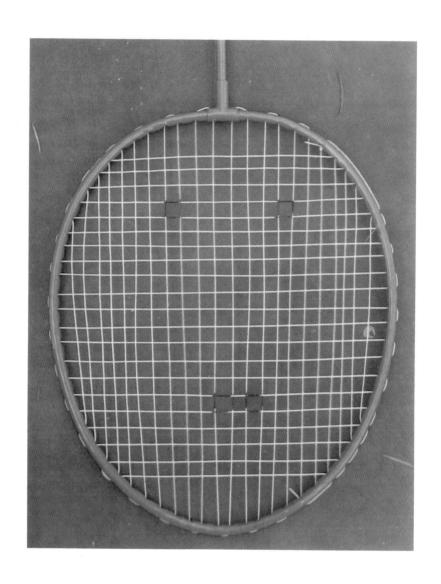

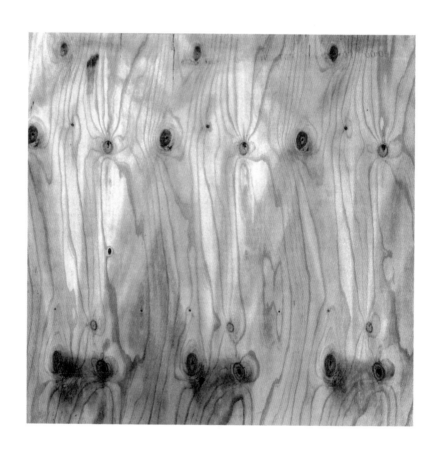

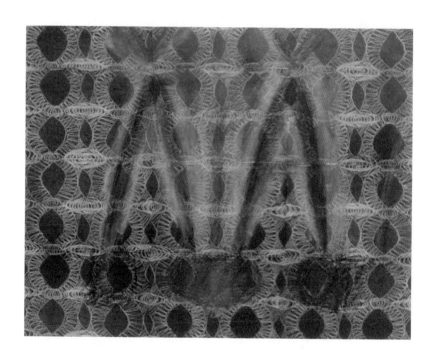

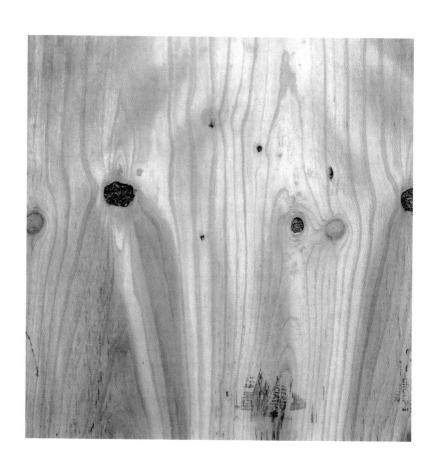

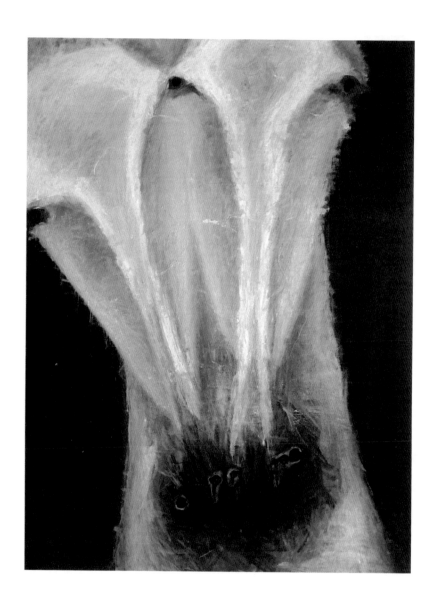

41

43

48

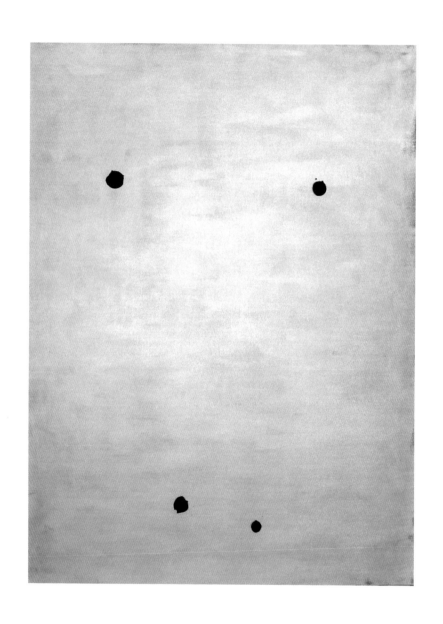

In Sok's view, back then he'd finally arrived at what he'd set out to find in his life journey of becoming the messiah, but even so, still had to spend many years working on putting it into words. As a part of this process, the above visual presentation was developed. Some of the paintings were already being exhibited in a Vancouver gallery. The entire presentation was designed to simulate his experiment. First he randomly threw some black paint on an empty canvas, believing the answer to his questions would come to him. That in itself was something he'd never done before. Although his entire life path had been rediscovering the *unknown-trust cycle*, he'd never actually tried just trusting in the *unknown*, like a born sorcerer who's wasted his whole life looking for magic power without ever attempting to command a pumpkin to turn into a coach. After throwing the black paint, Sok sat back and stared at the canvas. Considering his tendency to believe in the impossible, it wasn't a huge stretch for Sok to try this. Nevertheless, since he didn't have any idea what he was looking for, he was constantly trying to avoid seeing the predictable, just as people will invariably interpret *four dots* as being exactly that— four dots.

Before going any further, there's one correction Sok wants to make concerning the creation of the *Four Dots* painting that he deliberately created to use as a demonstration. His initial intention was to put together a Disneyfied presentation for quick and easy understanding. Next is the real version. Over the following pages, Sok's three original paintings are displayed.

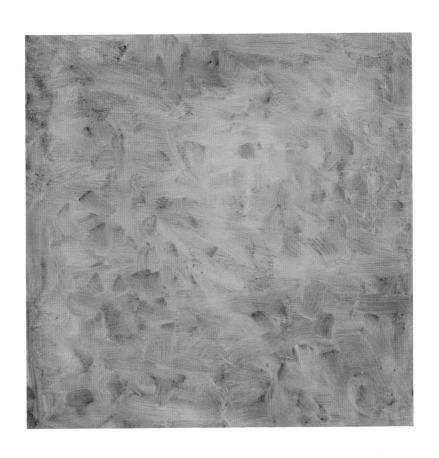

Instead of throwing some black paint on the canvas, Sok mixed half black and half matt medium. He chose the medium to thin the paint so that he could carelessly paint in a one-go-fashion. Then he covered the canvas with it and waited until it was half dry. As he happened to have a tub of black, a tub of white and other colours in tubes, this time he mixed half white and half the medium, painting it over the black just barely to cover it.

After painting the canvas grey, Sok sat and stared at it. Since he didn't know what he was looking for, he constantly avoided seeing the predictable such as recognizing it as a *messy grey* painting. Soon he started seeing things like a monster or a boat and etched them with a needlepoint on the canvas before it was dry. Sok already had a life practice of detached seeing, which had evolved out of his distrust for his environment. As he always sees with an extra layer of consciousness, for him what something seems to be is not always what it seems. He's become good at holding his vision without falling into habitual recognition mode. This ability stems from his suffocation trauma of never being able to trust what an image appears to be. Moreover, like a cat watching a leaf with the absolute certainty that it will eventually move if it waits long enough, Sok's learned to see in a state of suspension.

After about an hour of suspended watching and anticipation, Sok started seeing white horses on the canvas, dozens and dozens of them, as if the hosts of horses were pulsing in a white cloud towards him. A person might have a hard time *seeing horses* in the original paintings, since he doesn't have any reason to try for an hour and lacks the motivation of becoming the messiah. Sok did two more paintings in the same way. Even before picking up the brush to paint the second and third paintings, Sok already knew he'd get white horses, hundreds of them, even if he was painting with his eyes closed. It was like magic to be able to paint without a doubt as to the outcome. However, after *seeing horses* in his three paintings he still couldn't imagine how this sudden breakthrough could possibly provide all the answers.

In his visual presentation, Sok's attempting to convey all that happened that afternoon of *Seeing Horses*. The experience can be divided into three stages:

1. First is contemplating painting the grey canvas, which happens before *Seeing Horses*. It's like a person watching two dust particles bouncing towards each other against the sunlight and wondering whether he's in any way influencing their motion. To know that he has to influence them first, like pointing a magic wand and then waiting for the outcome;

2. That's the decision in the second stage of painting the grey canvas with the intention he'll end up painting the answer he's been seeking. But regardless of the potential outcome, when he's still in the first stage of not yet painting, there's another question as to whether or not the pure intention behind his input matters: *What if at the crucial moment his focus is divided between his belief in his power to manifest and his own personal doubt? Isn't it precisely this doubt that's the reason human beings can't move matter with their thoughts? Wouldn't it be possible to change the outcome if a person were able to quell all his doubts?* According to Sok, the only way to begin to answer these questions is to achieve a state of no doubt and then see what the output will be. He ponders, *But how do I achieve a state of no doubt? Has anyone done it so that I can share the experience with someone else?* Even if a person claims he's experienced a state of no doubt, unless it can be grasped as proof of how he got all the mysterious swellings all over his body, like capturing a bedbug, he'd still doubt as to whether or not he'd really achieved that state. Therefore, a person can't experience that doubtless state for the first time without having had a prior experience with which to compare as a reference; unfortunately, that would necessitate another previous experience, and so on. It simply seemed impossible to bypass this conundrum. Sok might order himself, *Just stop doubting!* But in order to obey this command he'd have to remind himself to stop doubting, which is it itself a thinking process of judging how at this very moment he's been doubting. Conversely, giving oneself a reminder to *stop doubting* becomes the next sequence of the doubting process which requires yet another reminder to *stop doubting*. Inevitably it becomes doubting, doubting, doubting, ad infinitum, like meditation with its incessant internal chant of *just stop thinking*. Simply it's not always possible to force oneself to achieve this state;

3. Nevertheless, Sok's created a set up that doesn't allow for any possible doubting in the third stage. The only way to eliminate all doubt is to engage in the act of *allowing*, even though action (being active) and *allowing* (being passive) might at first seem contradictory. The act of *allowing* is like the gesture of a person holding up his hand to feel the first drop of rain that he believes will at a crucial point fall on his palm after months of drought. Only an action devoid of *allowing* creates doubt and regret as to whether it's sufficient or correct. On the other hand, pure *allowing* without any action leads to waiting forever passively in the mode of relying on luck or coincidence. Living according to the desire for luck creates doubt as to how deserving a person is. Quite the opposite, *Seeing Horses* is an experiment in the act of *allowing*, which initially includes the input of

Sok's action of painting the grey canvas, and next involves the output of *allowing* whatever to come, which in Sok's case, manifested in *Seeing Horses*. For Sok, *Seeing Horses* signifies being in a state of no doubt while taking part in the act of *allowing*.

In hindsight Sok's realized that all his past attempts to become the messiah have stemmed from his masculine drive and have been based on doubt and lack of trust. His deep-rooted insecurity was what made him think that unless he worked like a slave, nothing would ever work out; on the other hand, he has to admit that without his drive he'd never have come to *See Horses* and get to the point of no longer having any doubts. He's always been aware of the destructive potential of his killing urge. Nevertheless, during his lockup, instead of destroying himself he learned to flip his energy like a bullfighter to convert it. Compelled by his masculine drive and arrogant rebelliousness, he finally said, *Fuck it!* to that same masculine energy and succeeded in elevating himself from being a seeker involved in the act of looking for answers to becoming a *seer allowing* his own answers to manifest. In this way his lifelong drive, originally powered by extreme distrustfulness, was transmuted into something he'd never fathomed. Instead of forcing something to happen, he'd simply *allowed* it. It was as if suddenly after years of constant struggling he no longer had to strive; instead he'd learned to channel that same energy to a place of no doubt and manifest it in the form of *Seeing Horses*. Furthermore, from his input of not doubting he got the output of knowing he'd experienced a state of no doubt through the physical and mental reference of *Seeing Horses*; like a bedbug, he'd reached a point where he no longer wondered if he'd really experienced a state of no doubt. Without needing any prior experience of having no doubt to compare it with, he was finally able to recognize it.

According to Sok, the state of no doubt can almost be achieved by anyone at any time. However, usually people aren't *aware* they're experiencing it. That's because without both a physical and mental reference point such as *Seeing Horses* there'll always be some niggling doubt, which means it's still a state of doubt, and they've lost the original physical feeling in the process of doubting. But Sok's been able to isolate that state and manifest it with the body-tuning device of *Seeing Horses* as his visual and physical reference point. Since then he's been able to conjure it up any time.

For Sok, *Seeing Horses* has explained all his life questions, one of which is to discover how it's situated at the core of existence. This will be explored in the *Second Canvas*. Furthermore, the ramification is that once it's clear, a person views it as a life and death matter. This concept will be developed in the *Third Canvas* by delving into the structure of *Seeing Horses*. Through *Seeing Horses*, Sok regained his childhood innocence, like King Arthur pulling the sword out of the stone, although in Sok's case, he chose to set up the sword and the stone for himself instead of accidentally running into it. After, he knew he'd never lose it again. He was moved to discover that the truth about the universe is wrapped in such a simple act, like a tiny seed encapsulating all the information of a big tree, miraculous in comparison to the grand production of shooting rockets into outer space. *Seeing Horses* is an activity any person can achieve, and is Sok's way of returning to his original childhood innocence. It's a little seed containing the DNA of the *unknown-trust cycle*. It's his homecoming.

Second Canvas: **Moonlight Under Snow-Covered Roofs**

After *Seeing Horses*, Sok's occasionally asked, *In order for* **Seeing Horses** *to be proof of who I say I am, shouldn't I be able to demonstrate that when in the state of choosing the **unknown**, anyone should be able to* **See Horses** *just like I do? But wouldn't it be possible that another person who achieves the same state might undeniably claim he* **sees** *something other than* **horses**?

For a few years, Sok struggled with his doubt as to whether *Seeing Horses* definitely shows he's doubtlessly believed. Of course he knows what he experienced, but also that verifying it might be a different story. In order to substantiate his experience, Sok reflects on his past when he used to spend the dominant portion of his waking hours staring at wallpaper as if he were locked up in a mental hospital. He'd gaze at the images until they became 3D and started moving.

After Sok dropped out of high school, he spent many hours in his bed. During the time when he was living in the single room he and his sister rented, he was often forced to starve for many days, which he found gave him a sharper sense of *seeing*. Lying in his bed, he'd imagine scenarios opposite from his reality. He'd figure out specific details such as designing in his head the floor map of a house in which he'd like to live, furniture to go in the house, the objects that went into the drawers. He'd contemplate the textures of fabric, cuts of cloth and designs of clothing, as well as speculate on the appearance, shapes and personalities of women, friends and foes, as well as the angles and movements of bodies. Always hungry, in his imagination he'd explore the smells and textures of food, what went into the food and how it was cooked. He'd then move into the plot, playing it in his head like a movie. As time went by, he was able to orchestrate everything all at once into a 3D vision in front of him in order to make it real and play it according to the storyline of his choice, which he was able to access readily from his fantasy archives.

Wallpaper 1

Wallpaper 2

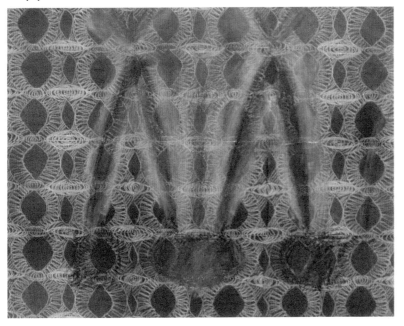

Even as an adult, Sok's spent a great deal of his life in bed, either staring blankly or imagining. This is because when he was growing up, he either felt abandoned, grounded, starving or sick. When he was ill he'd hallucinate, which heightened his senses and made him especially perceptive to sight, smell and sound. In his long periods of solitude he developed the ability to self-generate his hallucinations or was sometimes thrown into that state during his frequent bouts of sickness caused by the carbon monoxide poisoning he was exposed to everyday for more than six months a year. During the winters when his family heated the old Korean-style floors of their apartment that often had holes and cracks that leaked gases from the coal blocks, sometimes Sok and his sister would wake up dizzy and sick in the mornings and feel faint when they stood up. Sok was also regularly exposed to other chemicals such as insecticides and fumigation, heavy metals like mercury and lead in the objects with which he played, as well as the antibiotics and other medicines such as pain *killers* and parasite pills that he and his sister thought tasted like caramels. Looking back on his childhood, Sok's often wondered, *Why was I unable to **See Horses** back then under those highly toxic conditions during my frequent blank states of staring?*

Sok's pinpointed the moment of *Seeing Horses* as the seed containing all the necessary information. Later on after years of struggling, he realized that the answer to why he'd been unable to *See Horses* earlier lay in his adult willingness to choose the *unknown* in the instant of *Seeing Horses*. It dawned on him that in that state, *Seeing Horses* is the first and easiest thing that comes, whereas in his past experience of blankly staring at walls, although he had an inkling of the *unknown* back then, he made no conscious choice to surrender himself to it because at that time he was just randomly staring at the wall without the framework of deliberately setting himself up to do it. With this insight, Sok began to see that *Seeing Horses* is inevitable if a person makes the choice to enter into the new framework of the *unknown*.

During the period after *Seeing Horses*, Sok knew how important it was for him finally to be able to claim himself as a person. While he was preparing his coming-out-of-the closet debut, he was able to analyze and divide the procedure into a few steps to demonstrate the inevitability of *Seeing Horses*:

1. Sok has experienced two kinds of *seeing*: his normal mode of viewing and his *3D staring-at-wallpaper-until-it-moves* kind of *seeing*. The first involves memory. When Sok sees an apple, for example, he has to know that what he's seeing is an apple. Otherwise he'd freak out, exclaiming,

What's that thing? Is it from a UFO? But he wonders, *How did I see my first apple for it to become a memory of my first apple?* The answer opens a window to the second kind of *seeing* that involves neither memory nor expectation, in which *seeing* is perceived as a feeling of awe. In retrospect, the sensitivities Sok developed from his sicknesses and hallucinatory states elevated him from the usual cognitive mode of seeing an apple through memory recognition and gave him the ability to perceive three dimensionally, like the vibrational function of a video game.

What gave Sok this glimpse of clarity into the dualism of *seeing* were his paintings. During his two-year-lockup in his apartment that culminated in *Seeing Horses*, he painted. He had two purposes: first, he wanted to paint something that employed his sense of 3D vision; and second, he was attempting to kill the long hours of complete boredom. One of his paintings, *Moonlight Under Snow-covered Roofs*, demonstrates this dualistic way of *seeing*. The painting is on the next page.

When observing the two-dimensional surface of the painting, which contains many painted lines, the fact of the matter is that it's still two-dimensional, as are all paintings. But if the viewer lets go of that initial recognition of a bunch of lines and views with an intensity of focus that generates a strong feeling, *Moonlight Under Snow-covered Roofs* can all of a sudden be *seen* in distinctive 3D. Sok's experienced that this shift in modes of *seeing* occurs with a slight vertigo. He thinks this sensation comes from the fast drain of blood shooting from his brain down to the feeling-based kundalini in his ass.

While Sok was creating the painting, he painted the shadowed side of the roofs in darker lines on the white canvas as the first layer. He had to focus intensely in order first to *see* and then transfer the darkest part of the roofs in 3D from his head to the empty canvas. Since he wasn't painting from a photo image, which involves the first mode of thought-based seeing, his process in the second mode of *seeing* gave him a physical sensation. While painting a whole city of roofs in his focused mode of *seeing* with intense 3D feeling, he was able to quiet down his thoughts and witness the external manifestation of his inner 3D vision painted on the canvas.

If it's true that before actually painting Sok really saw the whole city of snow-covered roofs through his internal 3D vision, then the painting itself is a window into his inward vision. The difference between his inner vision that materialized onto the canvas and looking out a real window onto a sea of real snow-covered roofs is that the former's virtual and the latter's real. If it's true that Sok can virtually *see* the city in 3D,

then all the tiny roofs around the top edge of the painting should still be clear and visible, just as a person looking out a real window can see the roofs at a far distance from himself by adjusting his visual focus. As an example, let's say a person is taking a photo of a cat a few metres away. Against the clear image of the real cat, the photo would have a certain overall fuzzy quality because of the unfocussed images of far away objects in the photo such as the distant trees. On the other hand, unlike the 2D photo of the cat in front of the background of fuzzy trees, with his 3D insight Sok's capable of capturing the detail of the distant trees by zeroing in on them with his vision as if he's not looking at the foregrounding cat. In this way, while painting *Moonlight Under Snow-covered Roofs*, Sok zeros in on the distant roofs to *see* them just as if he were viewing a real city out a window. Sok's painting sheds light on the difference between 2D and 3D vision. According to Sok, as in the apple examples, the difference is the presence of the *feeling*.

Sok's found the *feeling* derived from music generates a similar 3D ability. With his sight and sound sensitivity, a small sound constitutes a space, like a tiny explosion. He can apply a similar concept within the realm of visual perception, in the sense that *seeing* wallpaper in 3D is different from looking at actual wallpaper. As an example, when the eight notes of the musical scale from *Do, Rae, Mi* to the next *Do* are heard, the *feeling* aroused can produce what Sok calls a *quantum* vision of a staircase, similar to imagining a train disappearing while the sound of it wears off in the dark. As the *feeling* fades, the listener's left with an inner 3D vision of *seeing* the train getting smaller and smaller as it disappears into the horizon. On a piano when the eight notes from *Do* to *Do* are played with an interval of a minute or even longer between each note, unless Sok can hold the *feeling* for eight minutes he'll not be able to *see* the staircase, since the previous notes are long gone by the time the next note is played because the *feeling*'s too weak to have the 3D thing going. Sok's noticed that the stronger his *feelings* are, the easier it becomes for him to summon a 3D vision. With his understanding of 3D vision being *feeling*-based, he's able to establish this as the first step towards grasping the inevitability of *Seeing Horses*;

2. This 3D insight can be applied to *Seeing Horses*. When Sok sees eyes or eye-like objects such as dots or any shapes with the contrast of shade, as in the case of the surface of his three grey paintings, he also has a choice between seeing them in the first cognitive mode of ordinary seeing or *seeing* them within the realm of the *unknown*, which generates the strongest *feeling*, like facing death. However, when he employs thinking through the first mode of memory recognition rather than the second

mode of *feeling*, he sees them in only two dimensions as typical two-eyed faces, like monsters. Sok had that experience briefly when he was facing the first grey canvas. At that time while he was still searching within the realm of the *known*, he'd sometimes see a monster or a boat; however, gradually as he went deeper into the *unknown*, he was able to lock into its strong *feeling*. Eventually, he saw *horses'* faces in 3D. *Why?* Sok's pondered. Later on he observed that within the *feeling* of the *unknown* in the second mode of *seeing*, it's possible to *see* the construction of 3D horses' faces in any combination with any four dots of any size in any configuration. For instance, if the two bottom dots are large and the two top dots are tiny, Sok *sees* a horse from the 3D angle of his eyes being close to the horse's nostrils and far from the horse's eyes, like a photo taken with a convex effect almost touching the nostrils. If the two top dots are large and the two bottom ones are small, Sok's eyes are close to the horse's eyes, as if he's looking down at the horses' face from a roof at a vertical angle. If one eye and one nostril are big, he's looking at them from the side. Moreover, the differences in the sizes of the dots and their distance relationships to each other constitute depth, which gives them 3D distance, just as two trees of the same height but at different distances make the more distant tree appear an inch long while the one close-up appears several feet long. Next are the visual examples:

2D *seeing*

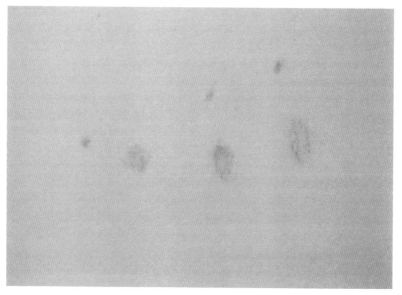

3D *seeing*

With the momentum of *Seeing Horses* through a strong *feeling* of the *unknown*, like a powerful engine, Sok *saw horses* from three, two and even one dot, making his own random configurations from every dot or slight shade to create the effect of a host of horses pulsing. In support of the argument that anybody dwelling in the state of the *unknown* would *See Horses* rather than some other image, Sok posits that it's more difficult not to *See Horses* from dots or shades than to *see* them, as long as the viewer persists in choosing to remain within the realm of the *unknown*. But the question arises as to why initially Sok *sees* eyes or eye-like objects, regardless of whether or not he has a strong *feeling*. Once again he inquires, *What if someone **sees** something other than eyes?* Sok tackled the problem by probing further into the impulse of *seeing*, which he's been able to link with his 3D ability to *See Horses*;

3. Sok's discovered the answer also lies in the presence of a strong *feeling* of the *unknown*. When he has absolutely no expectation as to what he'll *see* or experience, the *feeling* of the *unknown* doesn't mutate into thought process. In that state, Sok unconsciously scans in search of eyes or eye-like objects created in shade contrast on the *grey canvases* because of his habitual impulse to lock his eyes physically and emotionally into those of others.

Sok's experienced that *seeing* into another set of eyes triggers either fear or love. He feels uncomfortable looking into the eyes of others except that he's obsessed with being *seen* by their eyes, like an attraction to performing on stage in front of thousands of eyes. Sometimes in public Sok notices he's being watched by someone's eyes watching his eyes watching her eyes that are a bridge to knowing her actions are caught by his actions that are caught by her action of using her eyes to know his eyes are *seeing* her eyes *seeing* his. They become a window into *seeing* himself and her at the same time to create a connection, so that his thoughts are revealed as hers and vice versa. It's like *seeing* himself *seeing* himself behind a mirror, yet more intense, since it isn't virtual. In this ping pong rally of *seeing* her eyes *seeing* his eyes *seeing* hers, his thought inevitably dissipates and he feels disconnected with the temporal thought movement. This death of thought brings out *feelings* he envisions as being hers as well, but it can be awkward losing the train of thought. That he and she are in the same state that their thought can't move on provides them with the sensation of shared *feeling*, like love at first sight. Sok's experienced this can be frightening in his or her nakedness, yet at the same time irresistible in that he's drawn towards the *feeling* of not being alone. Sok's also found that his impulse of desiring to be *seen* by others extends to the eyes of animals and eye-like objects such as the headlights of cars. He's had the insight that inevitably human beings scan their environment in search of eyes even when there are none, ending up locking into eye-like objects. Sok thinks this behaviour stems from feeling separated at birth because when a person is birthed into the *unknown*, he feels he's been taken away from his mother. Sok's also observed that this desire to lock eyes is stronger among human beings than animals, due to people's lost feeling of trust and sense of abandonment. Therefore, Sok would say that the human feeling of insecurity concerning existence that causes people to crave being connected to others by *seeing* eyes is inevitable.

By applying this understanding to the previous 3D theory of *seeing* in parts 1 and 2, Sok's been able to grasp the inevitability of *Seeing Horses*. When the *seer's* in the state of the *unknown* and his vision switches to 3D, it's this built-in impulse to *see* eyes that causes him to lock into two sets of eyes, or *four dots*, to *See Horses*. In addition, Sok's found an additional element involved in the mechanics of *Seeing Horses*.

4. Sok initially assumed that the state of *Seeing Horses* is comprised of only two elements: *Thought* and *Feeling*. *Thought* is one frame of an image within the process of the first mode of seeing that requires prior

memory to recognize that what the *seer* is apprehending is an apple. *Feeling* is behind the second mode of *seeing* the image of an apple as if for the first time. In that state of awe, the visual *feeling* is more like bodily sensation. However, Sok got to wondering, *Is this dualistic contrast or vibration between **Thought** and **Feeling** all there is to **Seeing Horses**?* Later he discovered there's another element needed to manifest the state.

To shed light on the inclusion of the third element, Sok uses an example of two guys, one homely and the other stunningly handsome, both stranded together on a deserted island since birth. He wonders whether they even know they look different, but realizes they can't possibly because that would require a third-person to reject the homely one by offering the handsome one a tasty fish. With the inclusion of a third-person, each of the three would then be able to compare himself with the other two in order to recognize himself as being both similar to and different from them. Sok calls the combination of *Thought* and *Feeling*, with the addition of this third element of *Awareness, Triple Contrast*.

When Sok enters the realm of *Triple Contrast* he's intensely focussed, using his visual *Thought* at the front of his brain, *Feeling* the *unknown* at the kundalini source around his ass and finding the third element of *Awareness* where his skull and vertebrae meet. *Triple Contrast* could be called *Trinity*, a word that comes from the *Bible*, except that Sok thinks Christians confuse *Trinity* by identifying it with an entity, God, whom Jesus called *the Father, the Son* of the entity, Jesus himself, and the *Holy Spirit*. However, in Sok's concept of *Trinity*, or *Triple Contrast*, he calls the father *Awareness*, the son *Thought*, and the holy spirit *Feeling*. The triangle of *Triple Contrast*, consisting of the three elements of *Thought, Feeling* and *Awareness* is the self-sufficient, basic component of everything. Often referred to as *oneness, Triple Contrast* merges all three elements and is a third-person perspective of both unity and separateness. When Sok's in *Triple Contrast*, he's in a state of detachment through which he can simultaneously *see, feel* and be *aware* of himself in his surroundings that become reflections of himself.

Sok's observed that being in the state of *Triple Contrast* is somewhat similar to the vibrating function in video games that blends feeling with illusion to make the images seem real. But even with their vibrating function, Sok believes that video games are at most a visual aid because without the viewer or *seer* himself combining all the elements to create a potential 3D vision, it simply doesn't work, in the same way that for there to be a contrast between brightness and darkness, there needs to be an observer.

In a similar manner, when Sok's in the state of facing the *unknown* and experiencing *Triple Contrast*, the triangle consists of *Awareness*, the *Feeling* of the *unknown* and the empty space where *Thought* used to be. In this merged state, nothing's left for him to think about since it's impossible even to conceive of the *unknown*. When the site of omnipresent *Awareness* is unhindered by the thinking process, which takes up the space of *Feeling* and *Awareness* in the triangle of *Triple Contrast*, the *Feeling* of the *unknown* is accepted. From the gap in the triangle, *Thought* from a different plane of *Awareness* spontaneously arises. In Sok's experience, this takes the form of a frozen *Thought* image witnessed by *Awareness* and amplified by *Feeling*. It's *Seeing Horses*, a seat at the centre of the universe.

Sok's come to the understanding that the self-sufficient *oneness* of *Triple Contrast* is the independent plane that a divided thinking self can't ever know. In that thinking mode of being broken off from *Triple Contrast*, and therefore, of losing the presencing *feeling* of the *unknown*, he'll never be able to achieve the state of *Seeing Horses*. In his attempts to achieve *oneness*, a person often looks for something that connects to the familiar, not realizing he can never grasp it through a recollection of what's *known*. As long as he's looking for something, which is a mode of thinking, he'll always break *Triple Contrast* and evade the *feeling* of the *unknown*, without which he simply can't engine 3D to *See Horses* in *Triple Contrast*. A person might seek *Trinity* within a system of religion, thinking of it as a godly trio like *The Three Musketeers*, but as long as he remains in thinking mode, achieving a state of *oneness* or *Triple Contrast* is simply impossible.

Over the years, the concept that's troubled Sok the most is *Awareness*. Unlike the *unknown* or *nothingness*, the birth-death-related state over which everyone is in denial, *Awareness* is generally accepted as a valid notion that everybody knows about and can agree on. He used to share that same collective understanding of *Awareness* as being a sense of existence or consciousness. *But what is it really?* at some point Sok started to wonder. Its common definition, as distinct from *Thoughts* and *Feelings*, always seemed fuzzy to him, inviting questions such as *Why and how do I have it? Where does it come from?* Even after *Seeing Horses*, the answers didn't seem so clear. On one hand, he conceived of *Awareness* as being the same as the *unknown* or *nothingness*, yet it was also slightly different. *How so?* he often pondered. Eventually, what clarified the dilemma was delving into the notion of *Triple Contrast*.

Sok considers the *unknown*, *nothingness* and *Awareness* to be alike in the sense that they all describe the origin of the universe. However, it opens up the question: *If **Awareness** is the origin of the universe, but also the same as **nothingness**, even if it's a sense of existence, how could it alone (in the state of **nothing**) know itself to exist without anything else around with which to be compared?* The presence of sound, for instance, requires silence. Or according to Sok's concept of *Triple Contrast*, as explained with regards to the three guys stranded on the deserted island, *Awareness* requires two additional elements for it to know it exists. Therefore, contrary to the collectively accepted concept of *Awareness* as being a sense of existence, the original, fundamental condition of *Awareness* actually can't be that. Conveniently, there are other words such as the *unknown* and *nothingness* that can be used to describe that state more accurately. *But how or when did people start conceiving of **Awareness**?*

Sok imagines that the original state of *nothingness*, the *unknown* or *Awareness* is close to a blind, deaf baby floating alone in a void. Although he exists, he doesn't know that he does, since he hasn't yet awakened himself into the sense of existence that requires two additional elements. Therefore, the difference between *nothingness* (the *unknown*) and *Awareness* is that *nothingness* as the origin of everything has the potential to become something such as the illusive material universe, the state of the unawakened baby, while what people understand as *Awareness* is the state of the baby who's awakened himself into *Triple Contrast*, which is the beginning of the universe.

How the baby as *Awareness* wakes himself up to know he exists in a state of consciousness is that he expands into three elements: *Awareness*, *Thought* and *Feeling*. To become three, *Awareness* breaks itself into deaf *Feeling* that arises out of sound vibration and blind *Thought* as an illusive image, like pure imagination. Sok calls the baby's attempt to shatter his sense of *Awareness* into the three elements *oneness* or *Triple Contrast*. Similar to the notion of a fish jumping out of water, the baby, in his former floating state that can be described as aloneness, boredom and curiosity, not that he would know what those are, divides his sense of *Awareness* into *Feeling* and *Seeing* to *feel* and *see* himself. It's close to having the attitude of *Fuck it* that's necessary to push oneself into the *unknown* with total self-abandon for no reason other than just to see what will happen. This act of faith is safe, not that he would've known that prior to his awakening act, since it's merely an illusive act of imagination. The worst-case scenario would be that he'd go back to his prior deaf-blind state of not knowing he exists, and so he has nothing to lose.

As the outcome of his act of faith, he gets to *see* himself in *Triple Contrast*, which resembles the incident when Sok tried to kill himself as a teenager. At that time, some divided part of himself wanted to take that same action as the baby to satisfy the other part of his self's curiosity about death. Another act of Sok's that resembled the baby was when he was a teenager lying alone in his room feeling lonely, bored and hungry, imagining an opposite situation to his reality in 3D as if it were real in front of him. In the case of the baby's act of imagination, he starts conjuring up a reality opposite to his condition of *nothingness*. Sok describes this as something like being inside a globed mirror room.

Sok imagines the inside of a ball with its concave round wall being an inverted mirror surface, while his *Awareness* self is a small outward-facing mirror ball in the center of the room, its convex outer surface being a mirror as well. It's a smaller mirror ball inside an inverted mirror ball. Sok pictures those mirror surfaces of the two globes as being all eyes: *Awareness* broken into a sense of *seeing* as an act of imagination. Such is the baby's act of imagination as it awakens itself into being. Unlike his former state of *nothingness*, which could be smaller than a spec since it's *nothing* after all, when he pushes forth, he instantaneously creates infinite space and reflections of himself, like booting a Mac with two perfectly facing 3D mirrors at equal distance to each other at every angle. Sok imagines it to resemble an atom with an orbiting electron. Sok also imagines that those two mirror balls are magnets, each with opposite poles to constitute distance and space, which is his *Awareness* broken out with a magnetic push-pull *feeling*.

Just as Sok fantasized amazing food when he was hungry, out of *nothingness* the baby summons infinity as the opposite of his current *nothingness* reality. Sok envisions that act to be the beginning of the universe, the *empty canvas* waiting to be filled in. According to Sok, *Awareness* is people's faint remembrance of *oneness* or *Triple Contrast*, like a fleeting dream. It's the physical memory of one round of the *unknown-trust cycle*, though unfortunately not only is it faint, but without a reference point such as *Triple Contrast* it's impossible to incite human beings to regain trust in the *unknown*. That's why Sok developed the concept of *Triple Contrast* using his own term that sounds like the name of a wrestler. In *Triple Contrast*, the *unknown-trust cycle* can be *felt* and *seen* in *Seeing Horses*, so that people can no longer deny their built-in *Awareness* as the origin of everything.

Compared to *Triple Contrast*, the popular meditation practice of alternating between thinking and not thinking, often described as a letting go of the thinking self, puts Sok to sleep. This is because he feels an absence of the strong *feeling* of the *unknown* he needs to generate the inevitability of *Seeing Horses*. *After all, what's so **unknown** and scary about sitting with a bunch of people on a floor meditating?* he adds. Alternatively, *Triple Contrast* wakes Sok up with a sensation of *deja vu*. Awakened in *Triple Contrast*, Sok can *see*, *feel* and be *aware* of himself and the universe as one. For Sok, *Triple Contrast* is *Seeing Horses*. *Seeing Horses* is the seed of the universe.

Third Canvas: **Airplane Crash on Fifth Avenue**

1 Framework

From early on Sok desperately needed to know whether his life circumstances might've been a matter of choice, rather than fluke accident or some power beyond his grasp such as god or the universe. He thought if things were going to be continuously shitty, he'd only be able to tolerate them if he knew they'd been his choice. As long as his life apparently dictated that he be a victim, prolonging it didn't interest him. The only real reason he continued to hang around was that he was always curious about *knowing* what was going on. But Sok understands that if someone with deep traumas like his prematurely buys into the belief that his fate's determined by god or luck, for instance, that person's more likely to rebel by going on a killing spree in the form of a high school shooting and then committing suicide in a rage against god, a system or luck that's fucked him up. Not wanting to take action based on mere judgment, over the years Sok's worked on pinpointing who or what has determined his life incidents such as the initial decision to be born as a human being on this planet. On the day of *Seeing Horses*, for the first time Sok made a choice to determine he could actually be the choice maker. *Seeing Horses* allowed him to realize that his life patterns were the result of his and nobody else's choice.

Sok's theory on the process of how this occurred begins as follows:

If the world only consisted of what was *known*, such as physical matter, it would support the idea that among random collisions everything's coincidental, like chemical reactions between two compounds. If that were the case, happenings in the world and in people's lives would be beyond human control, and people would be prone to believing in luck, which is more than often the case. At the end of day, people often have a tendency to fall back on luck or coincidence rather than believing in themselves. Sok asks, *What's the point in trying hard if dumb luck can take away all a person's lived and worked for, like losing everything in a tsunami?*

But if the influential factor over the material world is the *unknown* or *nothingness*, then the concept of coincidence is negated and everything becomes choice; *nothingness* can't collide with *nothingness* to trigger an accident as if it were a collision between two bodies of matter. *Does nothing contain any particles that would be able to bump into each other to cause an accident?* It follows that *nothing* can only exist in a state of *nothingness*, and for there to be *nothing*, not a thing should be there. Sok inquires, *In such a condition of complete nothingness, how would it be at all possible for any object or material to come into existence accidently without there having been a collision between two objects or materials? And how did those two things come into existence out of nothing in the first place? If all material in the universe is of a certain age, what existed a second before the first thing?* Everything has to be the result of choice. *Nothingness* is the origin that gives every object the option of returning to *nothing* at some point; therefore, everything eventually belongs to *nothing* in its ultimate comings and goings. Considering the universe is expanding, its history can be traced back to when it was smaller and eventually all the way back to *nothingness*. A person might ask, *If there's such a thing as nothingness, how come no one knows about it?* Sok thinks this would be the same as a person having first to make a choice in order to know there's the option of making a choice.

As mentioned in the last canvas, *nothingness* and the *unknown* describe the same state. They coexist silently in parallel with what's *known*. This is the state of detachment, like an unblinking statue, which no one can passively get to know about. With the development of science and anti-religious sentiment, a lot of people have come to support the idea that if there's no evidence, like proof of the existence of god or spirits, *nothingness* simply doesn't exist. However, Sok's been trying to recapture the essence of *nothingness* through *Triple Contrast* in *Seeing Horses*.

Sok explains that grasping the *unknown* is like being in the silent presence of the invisible man. The closest anyone's been to grasping the *unknowable* is speculation. Doubtful as he is, Sok hates speculation since it brings about more speculation with the addition of individual interpretations. Over the years since his suffocation trauma, Sok became so mistrusting and paranoid that he actually would've had to touch the rainbow for him to believe it was real. Similarly, he had to spray-paint the invisible man before he was able to relax.

Sok remembers that spray-painting the invisible man was like overcoming the problem of *seeing* the back of his own head. Although it's physically impossible, he saw the possibility of getting at it indirectly with two mirrors, or in this case, two elements: first, Sok needed to envision the presence of the invisible man; second, he chose to spray-paint to what seemed to be a void. These two elements combined constituted an act of faith, or the *unknown-trust cycle*. It's similar to the experience and behaviour of a child; unfortunately, when children grow up the *feeling* of trust is forgotten. Sok calls this act of faith embedded between these two elements the *framework*. The *framework* is what isolates the *unknown* into a capsule.

According to Sok, the *framework* is input and output (the outcome of a person reaping the fruit of his trust). It's like a boomerang in that what begins comes to an end, just as this sentence is being written with the confidence that it'll be finished. Like the cycle of sowing and reaping, it's a choice that yields an inevitable consequence so that a new choice can be made. The nature of a boomerang is that it has to come back to the thrower in order for him to choose to throw it again. The *framework* means coming full circle to *see* an overview of the whole movement, like *seeing* a circle of maze from the sky. It's a tool to *see* that everything's a choice.

A fitting example would be the limited life span that inevitably ends in death instead of becoming stuck forever in one reactionary mode or another. Like a matrix, the limited lifespan is the shadow of the *unknown* pointing towards death that brings with it an urgency to trust. It's like a ghost train track that gets laid out in a circle simultaneously to the train's moving around the track. For Sok the concept of *framework* in its smallest scale such as *Seeing Horses* is a capturing of the *unfathomable*, like a tupperware container that holds in *nothingness* as the air trapped inside.

To catch the *unknowable* with his net of *framework*, Sok first had to bring himself as closely as possible to its edge, like perching on the brink of a pond to catch a fish. For the *unknown* to be distilled, initially all that is *known* has to be negated, like draining the water out of the pond. Conveniently during his lockup, Sok was sick of everything. The first thing he wanted to do was annul all that he knew, including the entirety of his memory, learning and impulses, the lump sum of his past knowledge and of history. He positioned himself on top of his previous experience, usually recycling his past, but with the openness of being able to choose the *inconceivable*. When absolutely everything *known* is cast off, whatever follows is *unknown*. To that effect, in *Seeing Horses* Sok made a decisive act to let go of everything he'd *known* and *allow* the answer to come to him. His act of *allowing* was his first entering into the *unknown*, since not only had he never done it before, but also there was no way of knowing what would follow. In full anticipation of getting an answer, yet without any expectation of what the answer would be, he entered into the realm of the *unknown* or *nothingness*. Out of his conscious act of negation he got to know his subsequent physical state, and with the body-tuning reference of *Seeing Horses*, the *unknown* became *known* to him indirectly. *Seeing Horses* brought on a visceral state of *nothingness* in *Triple Contrast* that permitted him to enter into the physical state of no longer needing to think about doubting, while at the same time *allowing* him to recognize he was actually in a state of no doubt. Since then he's found he can reenter that state repeatedly at will with the intensity of *Seeing Horses*.

Sok argues that the *unknown* is a state of mind void of questioning or recognition. Prior to being in that state, however, the doubting, questioning, thinking person sees the world within his expectations of what's *known* and recognizes only the surface of the grey messy painting or the generally *known* aesthetic functions of paintings such as that they're beautiful or something interesting to display or purchase. But Sok's grey canvases aren't necessarily interesting enough to buy or sell. Rather they invite that thinking questioning person to let go of his skepticism and enter into a state of no doubt. He won't have any expectation of *Seeing Horses* since he hasn't yet experienced it. Ironically it's only at the point when all his querying is nullified that he's able to *allow* himself the experience.

Seeing Horses is the framing of the *unknowable*. It's been the answer to Sok's life quest to grasp the core of the universe. Sandwiched between his choice to nullify all that he *knows* and his subsequent remembrance of making that choice lies the *unknown*, like a piece of boloney between two slices of bread that hold the structure of the micro *framework*. The boloney is *Seeing Horses*, the embodiment of the *unknown*. Within this enveloping *framework*, Sok spray-paints the invisible man and at once gets to *see* and recognize him through the medium of *Seeing Horses*.

To the person claiming he can spray-paint the invisible man and *See Horses* accidentally, Sok would reply that even if that person did manage to *See Horses* coincidentally, he wouldn't necessarily grasp its implications. Without making the intentional choice of envisioning and spray-painting within the *framework*, even if the invisible man accidentally appeared, the person might never be sure that what he'd spray-painted was the invisible man. Even if he spray-painted the void and by chance ended up with the invisible man, as a human being he'd likely worship the materialized image as if it were some kind of god or manifestation of the supernatural. Sok insists that without the intention of the *framework*, all action remains within the realm of speculation. Only within the *framework* does the invisible man come to be recognizable, and in Sok's case, become embodied in the image of white horses. Sok has no doubt that the outcome of the *unknown* is *Seeing Horses*. *Seeing Horses* was his choice then and continues to be at every moment.

2 Ending

Is the world ending? Sok used to ponder, just as most people at this point in history will occasionally wonder. On top of the seemingly unmanageable complications the planet is undergoing in 2011, there have also been predictions based on the Mayan calendar that the end of the world, as people know it, will occur in 2012. Regardless of the accuracy of the Mayan predictions, according to Sok, *Seeing Horses* also addresses the inevitability of the ending in that it reveals the existence of a *framework* that comes to an end in a circle, like a boomerang. However, someone closely following Sok's argument might conclude that *Seeing Horses* also seems to have the potential to imply the opposite. He might add that the presencing of the *unknown* or *nothingness* derived from *Seeing Horses* suggests that in the realm of *nothingness* everything becomes choice rather than coincidence. His reasoning is that since *nothingness* doesn't collide with *nothingness* to trigger an accident, everything's a choice, as Sok has explained. For every choice there is an outcome. So the person asks, *What if I make the conclusive choice to continue on forever in one direction instead of ending with the world? Shouldn't it be possible if everything's a choice that comes with its own inevitable outcome?* Sok insists that's not possible.

Sok posits that if all animate and inanimate life forms, objects and materials have chosen to come into existence, it can be assumed that each choice maker has been free to make that choice. Sok contends that without returning to *nothingness* in the form of death or embracing the *unknown* with trust, the choice maker will travel eternally in the aftermath of his first choice. Eventually when his initial choice has been forgotten, he'll wander on accidentally forever, never comprehending why he's trapped in a linear time flow. Even if he wanted to terminate the everlasting consequences of his choice, he wouldn't be able to do so since it would contradict his initial choice. As a result, he drifts on aimlessly as a victim of his initial choice. Having no destination, and therefore, never receiving any returns from his potentially long forgotten initial choice, the choice maker, once a free entity, turns into a slave who no longer knows he has a choice and flounders choicelessly in an unintelligible world of coincidence. Resigned to the human condition, he's simply forgotten who he is.

If it were true that one choice could turn into a cessation of the freedom of choice, a choice becomes an eternal trap of losing freedom, and the choice maker becomes a slave who no longer feels the freedom to choose. *What would be the motivation of a free man to choose to be a slave forever as the outcome of exercising his freedom?* Sok jeers. On the other hand, he appreciates the intelligence in the design of returning to *nothingness* and death that comes from having a *framework* that always comes to an end. It's like entering a class in school with the guarantee of the bell ringing when it's time to leave. Knowing the *framework* can even make the most boring class tolerable.

For the choice maker to maintain his choice-making status, the path prompted by his choice has to return eventually to its origin in *nothingness* to complete the loop of his initial choice. The question becomes whether the homecoming will be through natural and unwanted death or through *Seeing Horses* prior to his physical death as his next physical transmutation. Since *Seeing Horses* revealed to Sok that he's the choice maker, it becomes a choice in itself to live as a choice maker who's free to choose. Even when a person dies and comes back with no memory of his former life, which is the human condition of not remembering each death is a transition in the *unknown-trust cycle*, he'll repeatedly live with the same perception of not wanting to die and remain forever circling around the same loop of history. He's just like unconceived sperm sharing the same DNA and repeatedly failing to fulfill their potential to become a fetus as the next transition.

Entering the new *framework* is like transforming from a fetus into a human being. Sok was only able to access it when as a last resort he chose to abandon his reality of not acknowledging the *framework*. Embarking on the new *framework* meant choosing to let go of his former life of mistrust in which he feared his destination and doubted how limited, accidental and transient he was. Now that he understands the *framework*, he feels more at ease knowing his life isn't hinging on mere coincidence, and that it's not a one time deal that goes on in linear time with or without him; instead he knows that any time he can start the new *framework*. *So what's there to worry about?* Sok gestures. Becoming aware of the possibility of choosing a new *framework* is the same as overcoming death. Christianity tried it with the concept of heaven, but Christians aren't choice makers, due to their theology of letting their imaginary God with his thuggy temper make all their decisions. It's like Sok's mom, who's had a virtual fear of ghosts all her life but hasn't ever even seen one and so has no real grounds for being afraid. Likewise, people fill their imaginations with all the familiar scary thoughts concerning the *unknown*. This is due to the fact that everyone's lost the memory of *the unknown-trust cycle* they experienced at birth.

Another reason people aren't able to access memories of their former lives is because they're not free choice makers. If they were able to remember past existences, they'd know there was a *framework* of each life and that death's an illusion. They become free, knowing that after death comes another life as an alternative to annihilation. However, just as a freeman can't be liberated by someone else because then he'd always be dependent on somebody other than himself for his freedom, a person has to make an active choice to become a choice maker, rather than waiting to regain his memory accidentally or for some phantom rescue by extraterrestrials in UFOs. For Sok grasping the new *framework* for the first time through *Seeing Horses* was like recovering the memory of *seeing* his former life maze with its infinite paths and corners from the omniscient point of view of the sky, in the sense that he could clearly *see* how it began and ended. Sok explains that awareness of the *framework* comes at the end of the *framework* a person's currently in.

Between the old and new *frameworks* lies the *unknown*, like a bridge. Sok's last memory within the old *framework* was that he chose the *unknown* and then experienced it in *Seeing Horses*. That's how he became aware he'd gone through it and knew he'd entered into the new *framework*. As with regaining memories of former lives, his first remembrance after landing in the new *framework* was that he'd faced the *unknown* and emerged from it fine into the new *framework*. Suddenly he was embarking on the journey of the new *framework* without any fear of the *unknown*, as if he were remembering how at the beginning of his life and his old *framework* he'd crossed over the threshold from being a fetus to being born as a baby. This gave him a new perception as he became detached from the uncertainty of the future to embark on a more trustful existence. The closest *feeling* is that of a kid who has no concerns about the future, or being born as Terminator with a grasp on the entire *framework* of how and why he became a human. Sok adds, *The pinch between the death of the old framework and the rebirth of a new one is* **Seeing Horses**. According to Sok, *Seeing Horses* is an almost simultaneous merging of the old and new *frameworks*.

Seeing Horses is dying without having to die. When Sok saw the *framework* to know the *framework*, he was still alive in his body so that instead of undergoing an individual physical death of completing one lifetime, he experienced it on a historical level to *see* the whole macro *framework* from *nothing* to *nothing*. If the goal of human history is to accept reverting to *nothing*, and therefore to regain lost trust, then it's no secret as to whom the choice maker is: Sok. In his new existence he resides in the state of having neither past nor future, since all inclinations towards knowing the *framework* have ceased. Now that he dwells in the present, he's no longer time bound. The *framework*'s now. It's *Seeing Horses*.

Sok apprehends that people are caught between being curious about the sensation of death and not really wanting to experience it, like a person knowing he has to cross the bridge of death in order to come home, yet not wanting to. This dilemma is reflected in people's fascination with virtual death such as being attracted to watching someone else die, as if that will bring them the experience of death without actually having to die.

Next is one of Sok's paintings, *Airplane Crash on 5ᵗʰ Avenue*. Standing with their noses pressed against the interior glass walls of the building structures, the identical human forms photocopied in different sizes watching the crash depict people's irresistible desire to experience virtual death. Sok envisions himself somewhere, observing all the spectators in the buildings. He imagines he didn't get to see the airplane crashing down and is

standing in a place where he can't see the crash site. Nevertheless, he knows people have died by observing the reactions of the spectators.

3 The Rider

Sok's the heir of a family of mass murderers. His most immediate mass murdering blood connection was passed down to him from an uncle he never met named Bong Hun. Nevertheless, Sok's always associated himself with Bong Hun through family stories he heard from his dad and other relatives; Bong Hun was Sok's dad's oldest brother and a leading member of the Lim clan. According to what was passed down to Sok, Bong Hun shared the responsibility for the Korean War with his other Communist comrades. He had a lifelong revolutionary ambition to bring down the hierarchy of the ancient Korean feudal system that had recently been reinforced during the Japanese colonization. He was responsible for importing communism to the country and ended up risking more than two million lives for a revolution he deemed necessary. He assumed he had the right to decide what he wanted for himself, his family and the rest of Koreans, regardless of the human toll. His Communist involvement led up to the Korean War.

The Korean War happened a few years after Japan's surrender, prompted by the US dropping of the atomic bombs on Hiroshima and Nagasaki in response to the Japanese attack on Pearl Harbor at the end of World War II. During the Second World War, Japan had colonized Korea in its attempt to take over all of Asia. Before the Japanese colonization of Korea, even though the Japanese had already demonstrated their aggressive intentions with their rifle power, something that was new to Koreans, Korea remained passive in defending itself. By then, like abused Korean children, the country was collectively traumatized and discouraged after being invaded many times. As a result, the Korean government made a decision to close its doors to the outside, rather than take an active stance by learning about new weapons technologies and concepts to keep up with the rest of the world. The lockup didn't work, and consequently, Japanese colonization lasted over thirty years until the overnight passive liberation of Korea that resulted from the fateful atomic bomb attacks on Hiroshima and Nagasaki. During the colonization a few Koreans showed an interest in Communism as a solution to gaining liberation, but for that Korea needed to ally itself with China and the Soviet Union, as if being free from Japanese bullying were an invitation to all the Chinese and Russian thugs. Accordingly, only a few years after the Japanese colonization ended, Korea was divided into North and South, which led into the

Korean War puppeteered by the USSR, China and the US, each with its own political and economic self-interests. The war lasted three years, ending up in a truce between North and South symbolized by a dividing line cutting across the country that's been there ever since. From then on Korea became the Cold War spot on the planet, a free-for-all for thugs from dominant countries to take advantage and thrive.

The scale and level of calamity during the Korean War inflicted considerable torture and abuse on Koreans, who'd already experienced countless invasions. It further cast them into the mould of a traumatized people accustomed to playing possum. This national character mould has driven Sok mad and compelled him to break free of his Korean-ness. Following in the footsteps of his family tradition, this drive to cut himself loose has become Sok's own personal revolution. He views the Korean War as a karmic boomerang that came back to him as if it were up to him to clean up his family mess. However, he didn't fully understand the origins of his own rebelliousness until much later when he came to recognize his own pursuit of paradise in his uncle's passionate revolutionary desire to create a better world. Since throughout history, and certainly in Korea, there hasn't ever been a successful revolution that didn't bring on further upheaval, Sok's often wondered if he'd prevail in his revolution. Over time this became his life quest. Despite his own desire to revolt, he was aware of the stigma attached to revolutions in that they've never worked. Rather, they transform the rebels into scapegoats and victims who sometimes even become touted by authorities as witches and devils to crank up antidotes for the rebellious urges in everyone. Therefore, in launching his own revolution Sok's had to ask why revolutions are generally unsuccessful. To pinpoint the cause of this chronic failure, he's backtraced human psychological history and discovered that the problem lies in the notion of betrayal.

Sok's insight that betrayal and revolution don't mix comes from the idea that revolution requires a group of like-minded people to be in cahoots; however, given Sok's naturally doubtful nature, he wonders whether complete trust is even possible among human beings. To comprehend this more clearly, he's felt the need to delve into the concept of betrayal. According to his understanding, betrayal is when one person expects another to fulfill an obligation of some kind. He's observed that when the person with the onus fails to oblige, the result is disappointment and mutual resentment. Sok's noticed this to be more acutely the case among family members. It begs the question: *What debt does one human being really have to another if coming into this life is everyone's choice?* In order to find the answer, Sok takes a look at a classic family betrayal recorded in the *Bible*: the story of Cain and Abel that sets the tone for the long succession of betrayals throughout history.

Out of jealousy and his own primitive reaction, Cain, one of Eve's sons, kills his brother, Abel, who's favoured by God. In this particular story God appears to act like a typical parent, favouring one kid, Abel, over the other, Cain. Finally God curses and at the same time protects Cain by exiling him to be a restless wanderer of the planet with the implication that the lessons Cain needs to learn will be stretched out over a long time. Subsequently, Cain becomes the forefather of a stigmatized bloodline. Out of this simplification of the biblical tale, Sok summons the question: *Is Cain the betrayer or the betrayed?* If he received less attention than his sibling from either God or his family, in keeping with the almost universal tradition of blessing a favoured son, usually the oldest, everyone including the one who's received better treatment, can't help feeling betrayed since technically speaking, no one's entirely capable of fulfilling another's expectations. Viewed in this light, Cain and Abel are equally betrayed by God or their parents, just as God or their parents also feel betrayed, and this will be the case as long as there exists the concept of betrayal. Sok's observed that a felt betrayal is always mutual. To take this reasoning further, he suspects that in many cases the motivation for human migratory spreading all over the planet must've also been prompted by betrayal.

Sok's often pondered, *If it's true that human beings originated in one place, why did they move? What motivated people of the past to migrate to different areas, especially when they wouldn't have been able to bring their houses, farms, cattle and household items with them?* Not only that, but it would've been less efficient to hunt in smaller numbers. Sok reasons that considering that uprooting one's livelihood to settle in a foreign land has always meant risking considerable discomfort, danger and even lives, in most cases, the incentive for upheaval would've had to be graver than mere curiosity, like being forced to move out for being the black sheep of the family. Sok finds it difficult to believe that in historical times resettling was initiated by adventurous spirit, rather than by family or community betrayal. Since even now there doesn't seem to be any family free from betrayal, everyone needs to feel fulfilled by other family members to be proud of being a deserving member of the family and feel good about himself, like having a president father or a spelling bee winner son. Considering this long, ongoing history of the family betrayer and betrayed, people must've felt the need to create borders between their lands so as not to have to encounter their betrayers ever again. Only in this way would they have been able to avoid killing each other, as in the story of Cain and Abel. Sok's occasionally pondered that betrayal could also often be one motive for having many children, especially among Asians who must've suffered ongoing betrayals to move such vast distances.

With other clans and tribes living within travelling distance, people would've felt insecure about potential dispute. In the case of conflicts arising with other tribes, it must have made sense to have many offspring, especially boys bearing the same clan name. As the sizes of the clans grew, their bordered-off lands became nations and their family and clan feuds turned into wars. As in the case of individual relationships, each nation must've always assumed the other nation to be the one with the obligation. This is the best explanation Sok's been able to come up with for the excessive population explosion of currently seven billion people on the planet, to the degree of being self-devastating.

Sok wonders what Cain's last dying wish would've been if he'd had a chance to reflect on his past. If at that time he'd been aware of the possibility of reincarnation and that the human goal should be to break free of betrayal traumas, *wouldn't he have regretted what he'd done and wanted to find a way to clean up his karmic mess that kept repeating itself life after life and generation after generation?* Sok imagines Cain would've tried to stage a revolution so there'd be no more betrayal by distributing equal shares of the fruits of the planet to everyone. *Might not the Cain/Abel dispute have been a land dispute intended to implement a communist system, for instance, as in Bong Hun's case?* If betrayal is the initial motivation behind revolution, any successful revolution simply shouldn't allow it. With Sok's new understanding of the *framework*, he imagines himself as one of Cain's offspring, destined to be linked to the bloodline of stigmatized wanderers working on revolutionizing such erroneous perceptions as there's such a thing as betrayal, there's no need to take responsibility and there's no way to make active choices, in order to wash off his guilt as heir of the mass murdering Lim clan. In that respect, Sok attributes his insight into his own revolution to his mass murderer uncle and the saga of his own family betrayals.

Bong Hun was the oldest son of four brothers, and Sok's dad was the youngest, with two younger sisters after him. Sok's dad speculated that the Lim clan probably originally came from Mongolia or possibly China since the Lim family name can be found today in China, Japan and Korea. His dad's guess about the family origin comes from shared behavioural characteristics between the Lim and the Mongols. The ancient Mongols were known for being a primitive, rebellious bunch, their dominant characteristics being riding horses and living wildly, rebelliously and freely. Sok guesses that for any Mongol or Chinese to move to a new place like Korea with the likelihood of having to learn a new language and becoming somebody else's servant, he must've been running away from a betrayal episode within his Mongolian clan. Regardless of whether or not the Lim clan actually came from Mongolia, Koreans bearing the family name of Lim lived under the limitations of being at the bottom end of the Korean feudal hierarchy, ranking under and serving noble families bearing famous Korean names such as Kim, Lee or Pak. The best bet for Lim clan members was to become independent farmers by buying off a piece of land if they were able to save anything in their capacity as servants. However, given the proud rebellious streak Sok's observed in himself and among more recent Lim clan members he's known or heard about, accepting low-ranking societal positions must've been humiliating and difficult. Sok finds it hard to imagine that someone would like to leave his house and cultivated land to face the *unknown* with the possibility of becoming someone else's servant. Sok's noticed that in their various ways, the whole Lim side of the family—his dad, uncles, aunts, sister and himself—have all shared an acute dissatisfaction with the Korean political, social and educational systems. It follows that the original Lim clan also wouldn't have been happy in the system they were born or came into, and that the seed of discontent must've burgeoned into revolutionary aspirations in later generations. Certainly around the time Bong Hun was actively involved in communism, the Lim clan's deeply rooted desire to be free and fair was distilled in him through bottomless support. The family ambition became especially strong while living under Japanese colonization during the Second World War when Bong Hun was in high school.

Despite his revolutionary spirit, Bong Hun was a gentle, spiritual soul who spent most of his high school years in the Korean central prison during the Japanese colonization. He was arrested many times based on allegations of being the brains behind the communist movement welling up in Korea. At the other end of the spectrum, Bong Hun was well-respected among Japanese police and prosecutors who were impressed by his guts and brilliance. Once a Japanese prosecutor told him he deserved to be a communist leader. Bong Hun saw an opportunity not only to force the Japanese out of the country, but also to bring equality to the Korean people, something the Lim clan had wanted for many generations of being at the low end of the feudal system. Members of the Lim clan couldn't put up with living under hegemony and didn't believe anyone else should have to tolerate being treated unjustly or unequally either.

When Bong Hun went to prison, his father put his best rice fields up for sale to bail him out. Sok's granddad, a self-made wealthy farmer, was willing to bestow everything he had towards his son's ambition and compassion for the Korean revolution. Although Sok's granddad adored all his kids, he had a huge respect for his eldest. When Korea was finally liberated from the Japanese after the atomic bomb attacks, Bong Hun was preparing to become mayor of Korea's capital city, Seoul, just before the onset of the Korean War that was already brewing. During that time, his brothers shared Bong Hun's ambition of becoming the ruling family of a new Korean elite.

Although Sok never got the chance to meet Bong Hun, he knew the other three Lim clan brothers, including his dad. If he had to describe their distinctive qualities, he'd choose one of his favourite stories of when his dad was in elementary school. One day Sok's dad ran into some money between the pages of a book he knew belonged to one of his older brothers. He took half of it and went to town to dine in one of the fancy Japanese restaurants he'd always wanted to try. For Koreans living under Japanese colonization, Japanese restaurants were of the most expensive and highest quality, and for the most part were inaccessible to ordinary Koreans. Even though he was just a kid, in fluent Japanese Sok's dad ordered many dishes that night while enjoying dining alone.

The Lim clan shared other qualities. They were audacious with neither a trace of apology nor hesitation in action, as well as inquisitive, straightforward and masterful at debate. They were a primitive bunch with sharp, penetrative eyes. Growing up Sok witnessed the power of his dad's gaze. People couldn't look him straight in the eye because he was too intimidating. His dad's first significant job was working for the Korean CIA, where unfortunately later on, due to his rebellious nature he had trouble with one of the influential generals in the military. Sok's dad had attempted to rescue the General's secretary who was being held captive in the military after serving her term because of the General's sexual interest in her. In the middle of the investigation, under the General's influence Sok's dad was fired and long afterwards continued to be sabotaged in his attempts to find employment. Years later after a long dry spell of not being able to find work, when Sok was in middle school his dad got a contract to work for a construction company. His role was to deter professional thugs who got in the way of highway construction; unfortunately, he was fired again because management found him too intimidating. Growing up Sok observed that like his dad, his Lim uncles all had similar behaviour and temperament. They possessed qualities that could have been put to good use leading Koreans, who've historically lacked initiative in changing their psychology and character as victims. The Lim clan was interested in balancing out the Korean tendency to retreat, as when the Korean government closed its doors to outsiders before the Japanese colonization, as if the whole country understood itself to be a metal safe in which the people could be locked in from the outside. In the Korean paranoid imagination, a general lockup from the world is the best way to remain safe, as if there's a governing party in heaven that has the omniscient power to force other nations to comply. Just in case that might be true, they've been emphasizing virtuousness by playing the good old possum. The question is: *Why after so many invasions would Koreans come to the conclusion that escapism's more effective than fighting back, unless their reasoning capability had been compromised by extreme emotional reaction, the result of post war syndrome?* The mass murdering Lim clan felt the need to make an executive decision for the rest of Koreans, proclaiming as do all revolutionaries: *Some people have to be sacrificed for the sake of the revolution!* In the process of trying to change their own circumstances, their crime was that they thought they had the right to determine the fates of everyone else.

During the time in which the Lim clan was engaging in the illegal activity of launching a revolution, family trust was everything. Their circumstances required absolute discretion. When in the preliminary stages of launching a revolution, family members are expected not to rat on other participants even when tortured or threatened. A similar phenomenon can be found in gangs such as Mafia families who enforce trust by executing any betrayers. By all accounts, the Lim clan was a loving, loyal family circle, until Bong Hun's bride entered the picture.

With the approach of the Korean War, Bong Hun took a prominent position in the Communist party and got to live in a luxurious traditional Japanese house in Seoul with a sizable tree growing in the middle of the living room where he frequently had his brothers over. He married a woman from what is now North Korea. To his brothers' amazement their sister in-law was the most stunningly beautiful woman they'd ever seen. Although she was supposedly Korean, by all accounts she looked exotically Russian, though no one would have ventured to guess at the details of her genealogy. Being at the centre of all that male attention, word had it that she seemed to find each of the Lim brothers attractive.

After the Korean War broke out, Bong Hun was dispatched from North Korean headquarters and became the mayor of Seoul, but at some point during the fury of the war he went missing. Around that time when Sok's dad was a high school student, the clan members were scattered, and some of them were hiding in temples. However, Sok's second uncle and his sister in-law ran into each other by chance somewhere and fell in love. They conducted their secret love affair amidst battles and starvation with no hope of tomorrow. Some time later, Sok's grandma walked in on them sleeping together and informed the rest of the family. The third brother and especially Sok's dad, who was the closest brother to Bong Hun, condemned the adultery as unacceptable and interpreted it as a family betrayal.

When the war ended, Bong Hun was still missing and was never found. The clan suspected he'd been killed by one of his Communist colleagues. It's a fact that Il Sung Kim, the North Korean Communist leader after the war, openly killed all of his competitors to gain power, later becoming one of the most ruthless dictators and maintaining a god-like hegemony until he died, at which point the leadership was carried on by his son, the current leader Jung Il Kim. If that were indeed the fate of Bong Hun, he must've felt betrayed by Il Sung Kim, who after all was his comrade. If speculation's true about how he died, Sok would say as a descendent of the bloodline of Cain, Bong Hun would've found himself standing in the shoes of Abel. In fact, towards the end of the war, everyone in the Lim clan must've felt betrayed by someone, either by family or friends, just as all South Koreans who had family, relatives and friends in North Korea must have experienced the same after the North Korean invasion. All were living as betrayed victims in the Korean Peninsula.

The three remaining brothers were never the same after the war, feuding until they died and focussing their revolutionary energies on harming their own kin. Sok reflects that had they not been so attached to all the Lim family dramas, the second brother and Bong Hun's wife could've eloped and lived happily together away from everyone, feigning being missing persons killed during the war. Even if they hadn't run away, the rest of the clan shouldn't have blamed them for the collapse of the family. After all, it was a respected Mongolian tradition for a man to look after his sister-in-law in the absence of his brother, and Bong Hun himself might have actually condoned it. Nonetheless, not reacting to family betrayal is generally unheard of everywhere, especially among members of the Lim clan whose built-in weakness contradicted their revolutionary convictions. At some point, the second uncle was pressured by his family to marry someone else with whom he had a son and a daughter, while his sister in-law lover lived under the same Lim clan roof with her daughter from her marriage with Bong Hun. In her precarious position she became a scapegoat of Lim clan hypocrisy. Nevertheless, the couple still discretely conducted their love affair away from the eyes of outsiders, though not necessarily from family scrutiny. The Lim family and the new wife lived out their lives in an atmosphere of anger and resentment, while publicly protecting their family secret of incest, adultery and betrayal. Like many Korean families, they continued to live unhappily together, not knowing how to untangle themselves from the mess they'd made. Bong Hun's wife found satisfaction in harassing Sok's mom, the wife of the brother who'd given her so much trouble. In this way the Lim family betrayal trauma was passed down to Sok, who received from his mother the gift of his own urge to launch a revolution devoid of betrayal. In fact, the Lim clan's mass murdering karma fell onto Sok, who's been an aversion for Koreans throughout his life. Furthermore, Sok's felt that the karma of Cain landed on him so that he could take historical responsibility for disturbing the shit.

After the war, the Lim clan spent a lot of the remaining family fortune getting rid of any record of Bong Hun. Under Korean national security laws, communists and their next three generations of descendants have been objects of government scrutiny and discrimination. As a result, now there are only a few witnesses left who know the story of Bong Hun. A little over a decade after the war, Sok's dad got married. The unfortunate thing about his dad marrying a Korean woman was that members of the postwar generations like Sok's mom wouldn't hesitate to sell out under any hint of pressure to avoid the kinds of peril they might have encountered during wartime. According to Sok's dad, Koreans had created a voluntary police state to rat on and persecute guys like him who challenged the system. He believed the reason government propaganda promoting blind patriotism was so effective in programming Koreans to rat on each other came from their war reaction of having been in constant fear of danger, which had conditioned them not to be able to think beyond their own immediate safety. Although Sok's dad had learned to take for granted a certain degree of disloyalty from just about everyone, the person who most represented the potential for betrayal was Sok's mom because she wasn't capable of handling any kind of stress. As a descendent of the Lim clan he simply didn't trust her, and in that sense it was a marriage made in hell, though from Sok's perspective, eventually they confronted one another with what each had to face.

Sok's mom has always been like a kid with little capacity to deal with traumas, yet at the same time she's always been attracted to adversity, and consequently, has met with a lot of crises in her life. It's true that like everyone else of her generation she's a product of war trauma; nevertheless, due to her unconscious, selfish, childlike responses to ordeals and suffering it still hasn't occurred to her, even in her later years, that throughout her entire life she's never stood up for anyone. In this regard, Sok's dad felt she was the furthest a person could possibly veer from Lim family standards, so much so that Sok often wondered why he'd married her. Sok also sensed, however, that early on she'd also had enough of the Lim family shit; of course, given her country naivety and tendency to freak out over the most trivial occurrences, having to live with her royal asshole husband meant she was bound to react. On the other hand, Sok's dad, who'd initially intended to set up a trusting family alliance in response to the family betrayal he'd experienced growing up as a member of the Lim clan during the war, ended up being just as disloyal to his own wife and family by fuzzing over the line between betrayer and betrayed. Nevertheless, upon meeting his future wife for the first time, Sok's dad thought she was pretty.

It's true that if Sok were to impart all the stories about his dad's atrocities, anyone would agree there's been no asshole like him throughout the whole history of mankind. It's also true that Sok's mom would've been a dream woman for most Korean men of her era in that she was beautiful, servile, good natured, fun loving, generous and tasteful. In another marriage she might've been the mother of kids who'd have sung, like Janis Joplin, that their *daddy's rich and their mama's good lookin'*. Just like everyone else, Sok's mom reacted to her surroundings. But really she's the most childlike person Sok's ever met, who throughout her life was pushed way beyond her limits by the Korean environment and her husband, who was not only incapable of seeing his own faults concerning everything, but also was the most destructively masculine person Sok's ever met. Growing up Sok was caught between the two extremes of his parents, both in their own ways exhibiting the psychological scars of postwar syndrome.

In addition to having to endure his self-inflicted, unhappy marital situation, Sok's dad felt that having a son like Sok, whom he mistakenly thought took more after his wife, was yet another betrayal since he'd been hoping for his only son and heir of the Lim clan to be more like him. What his dad hadn't realized was that all through Sok's childhood, Sok had also been undergoing unfair treatment because his dad had pretty much always dismissed his son's talent, sensitivity and more artistic nature in favour of his daughter, whom he believed took after him in that she possessed more obviously assertive Lim family characteristics. From Sok's perspective, however, while he was feeling betrayed by his dad, he was also secretly suffering from the betrayal of his mom. As a kid he was silently dealing with his own traumas without blaming anyone.

Back then Sok sided with his mom, recognizing that his dad was a problem in her life and desperately trying to protect her from his physical and verbal abuse and extreme psychological cruelty. Gradually out of rebellion against his dad he learned to suppress his Lim qualities. This ended up being the most significant factor in creating the ongoing tension between them, right up until his dad died in Sok's early twenties.

When Sok looks back on his past, he sees himself as Cain being reincarnated generation after generation with the desire to undo what he's done. He imagines that Cain's underlying guilt about killing his brother has finally manifested itself through Sok's quest for finding ways to restore peace and trust in the world. After Bong Hun's death, Sok grew up with the essence of Cain in that he was endowed with the insight that betrayal and revolution don't mix. It's only been in the last decade that Sok's been able to see how his mom's suffocation and his dad's favouritism had to happen. The abuse he received from his parents was enough of a fundamental betrayal to allow him to live without any expectation of not being deceived by anyone. Due to his mom's betrayal, he turned into an outsider no longer subject to betrayal. He became an island, totally focused on the void within himself.

Looking back Sok understands how his first uncle believed that regardless of the sacrifice and expense, he had to decide what was necessary, not only for himself but for all Koreans. What he didn't recognize was that unwelcome change under the name of revolution is itself a betrayal because it's a biased way of viewing the state another person or people are born into as being lacking in some way and in need of revolution. In that sense Bong Hun's revolution was a failure from the onset. This realization has prompted Sok to wonder how it'd be possible for him to stage a revolution that wouldn't fail. The solution came to him after *Seeing Horses*.

Upon *Seeing Horses* Sok perceived he'd had a breakthrough, yet at first he couldn't really grasp its ramifications. It occurred to him to look through the *Bible*. Sok's not religious, though he'd argue that nonreligious people are inevitably superstitious in the sense that they believe in luck and coincidence, rather than in themselves as choice makers. Sok has never completely trusted the *Bible* because he thinks it was manipulated to control humanity with the inclusion of a third omniscient presence, God. However, he also manages to be able to see through its narrative strategy and has found it to be a relevant archetypical guide to human psychology. That day after *Seeing Horses*, Sok opened the *Bible* he had with him during his two years of lockup to some part in the *Book of Revelation* and skipped through the headings of each chapter that were available in the particular version he had. It's not unusual for a guy like Sok to assign biblical significance to a matter that happened one afternoon, believing he'll discover himself in it. Inevitably, he found something in *Revelation 19*:

The Rider on the White Horse

11 I saw heaven standing open and there before me was a white horse, whose rider is called Faithful and True. With justice he judges and makes war.

12 His eyes are like blazing fire, and on his head are many crowns. He has a name written on him that no one knows but he himself.

13 He is dressed in a robe dipped in blood, and his name is the Word of God.

14 The armies of heaven were following him, riding on white horses and dressed in fine linen, white and clean.

15 Out of his mouth comes a sharp sword with which to strike down the nations. "He will rule them with an iron scepter." He treads the winepress of the fury of the wrath of God Almighty.

16 On his robe and on his thigh he has this name written, KING OF KINGS AND LORD OF LORDS.

17 And I saw an angel standing in the sun, who cried in a loud voice to all the birds flying in midair, "Come, gather together for the great supper of God;

18 so that you may eat the flesh of kings, generals, and mighty men, of horses and their riders, and the flesh of all people, free and slave, small and great.

19 Then I saw the beast and the kings of the earth and their armies gathered together to make war against the rider on the horse and his army.

20 But the beast was captured, and with him the false prophet who had performed the miraculous signs on his behalf. With these signs he had deluded those who had received the mark of the beast and worshiped his image. The two of them were thrown alive into the fiery lake of burning sulfur.

21 The rest of them were killed with the sword that came out of the mouth of the rider on the horse, and all the birds gorged themselves on their flesh.

Although Sok noticed the obvious parallel between the white horses in *Revelation 19* and the white horses he'd *seen* on the grey canvas, that wasn't what ultimately caught his attention. What he found most personally relevant was the line, *He has a name written on him that no one knows but he himself* (19:12). Sok immediately felt that nothing could describe his own dilemma better than that. Miraculously, it seemed to address his experience of never having had a role model who'd been able to launch a successful revolution. Sometimes Sok couldn't help but feel he was the only one wasting his life chasing the idea of successful reform that had so far never materialized. He felt he'd been facing the dilemma of becoming the first person *that no one knows but he himself* (19:12), as in the case of Galileo and his theory of the earth being round that sounded so ridiculous to everybody else at the time who was living happily on the flat earth. As in the case of Galileo, who fully experienced the quandary of being the first person to *see* the world in a particular way, Sok's felt the urge to let others know about *Seeing Horses*. He thinks it might be better explained through the concept of time.

Let's say someone was the first to have a new concept in the year 2000. If that were the case, he'd have newly grasped something that had been viewed differently by everyone else until that point. However, if time were to be backtraced from that point to the year 1995, for instance, no one including that first person would have any clue about his theory-to-be in 2000. In order for the first-person-to-be to make his own choice for a new perception-to-be, without having anyone to learn from, he'd have to rely only on himself so that he wouldn't have to worry about someone else misleading or betraying him. With no one to lean on, he'd break the barrier of what was *known* up to that point and burst forward with his new concept out of the *unknown*. That seemingly impossible action would be his choice to go for what wasn't yet *known*. In this way the first person chooses to become a choice maker; in Sok's case, he was the first person to *See Horses*.

Sok associates being the first person with being a mass murderer. The first responsibility of being the first person is to accept forever being the first person without necessarily having others around to share the experience. It's a lonely road. In Sok's case, it has entailed he go on without any expectation of being understood, since after all, he's the first person to claim to be the *Rider* in *Revelation 19*. Sok understands being the first person to mean making a choice to return to *nothingness* before his inevitable natural death, whereas most people's inaction reflects their not having made the conscious choice to embark on their new *framework*. Sok's had to accept the fact that there might not be anyone else who will choose to be a choice maker, since not only is it a difficult path, but also there seems to be too little time remaining. Nevertheless, he considers himself to be the brightest, darkest character to deliver his personal truth of being a mass murderer who's putting everyone else through a wine press with only his words. He's not up to failing his revolution by physically killing someone, an action he believes would only repeat Cain's saga of betrayal. For Sok it's simply a matter of joyously talking about the truth of his experience. The way he sees it is that how his words affect others isn't his problem because for him it's all a matter of individual choice. By *Seeing Horses* and then reading *Revelation 19*, Sok was able to confirm that accepting being the first person is his way of conducting his own successful revolution.

Unlike Bong Hun who sacrificed millions of Koreans for the sake of his own cause, by accepting the role of the first person conducting his own self-revolution Sok decides his own fate, while not interfering with that of others. It's true that his revolution finishes where his own body ends; nevertheless, his personal revolution won't necessarily fail on a collective level, since only one person is required to prevail in travelling the loop from Cain to Cain to clean up the Cain karma of human betrayal. Sok sees himself returning to Cain as the heir of an evil, stigmatized bloodline, like the numeric biblical symbol 666. In this way he completes the old macro *framework*, the entire human history of betrayal, to start a new one without any hint of it, since through the experience of having been betrayed at the most fundamental level, he's learned how to live without that aspect in his life. Sok's insights into the act of betrayal are the gift he's received from his parents, extended family and Korean up-bringing that has ultimately freed him from any feelings of guilt or obligation. The gaining of that crystal clarity is Sok's own personal revolution. Unlike Cain who was the first murderer, though Sok acknowledges Cain's desire to kill, like Dexter, Sok lives by his own code that he only kills with his *words*. In so doing, he chooses to dissolve the Lim clan tradition of family betrayal and begin a new *framework* of trust. *Seeing Horses* is setting the Lim clan and its Mongolian ancestors loose to run free with their horses all over the planet.

Throughout the process of *Seeing Horses* during his lockup, Sok didn't betray himself under the pressures of self-imposed starvation and survival. He's come to understand that he has the choice either to live with betrayal or not. Now for Sok, the only betrayal is self-betrayal, and as the first person he's made his choice to overcome it.

4 Multiple Characters

After painting the three grey canvases, Sok came to a vague understanding of the *framework*, which back then was more of a feeling-based perception than an intellectual understanding. He felt he'd broken through a barrier and come out with the knowledge that his reality was the outcome of his choice, and therefore, that there was nothing and no one to blame or depend on. He began to wash off the grime of religion, which he defines as the concept of tomorrow that was caked up over his life like an oil spill. Regardless of how slow and difficult the process, there was no one he could hold accountable except himself. What made it so difficult during the last leg of his two-year-lockup was that deep down he wanted a clean solution to his present life circumstances of living in a foreign country without any remaining money or connections. Understanding that no one would come to rescue him from his deserted island, rather than calling for help he thought he might as well pour his energies into something, one step at a time. So he continued working on his painting and writing. What he didn't realize was that he was still busy betraying himself, trapped within his built-in need for recognition. As ultimately he wanted to be appreciated, Sok had always been successful at convincing himself that what he was doing would eventually be acknowledged for its universal significance.

Meanwhile, life was going on and Sok had no idea that the completion of *Seeing Horses* through his *four dots* visual presentation and writing was going to take seven more years. On top of that, he didn't know that the point of it all would be finally to wash off his desire for recognition. Nevertheless, oblivious to the time and effort it would take, he went along working hard day after day always convincing himself he'd finish it within a few months. All the while he continued to fluctuate between being a *martyr* and a *killer*. Actually Sok's got multiple personalities. He's numbered them to be about twelve: *Killer, Martyr, Destroyer/Sabotager, Reasoner, Skeptic, Warrior, Believer, Hermit, Victim/Saviour, Hedonist, Junkie/ Addict* and *Clown*.

Killer and *Martyr* are at opposite poles, but similar. When they ally themselves they have limitless power; *Killer* wants to kill and *Martyr*'s willing to accept the consequences of *Killer*'s actions by desiring and allowing himself to be killed. Both having accepted the other extreme, neither feels he has anything to lose. Concerning their marriage, *Warrior* works on their behalf with his perpetual masculine drive. Like a loyal servant, he's effective and responsive to traumatic events. However, when he becomes stuck in his endeavours, *Destroyer/Sabotager* comes along to end the *framework*, initiating a death cycle and with his magic touch turning everything to ashes. He's a solider of progress, the one who makes it possible for Sok to cover a lot of distance in his life. However, his dramatic acts inevitably bring about one failure after another.

Tired of never having any success, *Skeptic* sarcastically enters the picture. Although critical of *Destroyer/Sabotager*, *Skeptic* wants him to remain active since as long as there's ongoing failure he can continue to enjoy complaining in his role as one of the dominant characters.

Skeptic keeps the balance with *Believer* who can naively go on waiting forever for the ship to come in. His childlike innocence plays an important role in Sok's life, but when he joins with *Victim/Saviour* they dither in a state of inactivity. *Victim/Saviour*'s the lowest of all Sok's characters. He's caught between allowing himself to be abused and at the same time being resentful. Instead of looking at himself, he flips everything to make it seem that in order to stop the abuse everyone else is in need of serious help. He constantly has to be stabilized by *Destroyer/Sabotager* and *Skeptic*.

Reasoner's the only one who actually listens to *Skeptic*. Unlike *Believer*, *Reasoner*'s grounded in his sharp sense of reality and doesn't allow for any mysticism. For him everything has to make sense. Sok considers *Reasoner* to be his capable butler or secretary who has slight authority over the other characters. Meanwhile, like a harsh teacher *Skeptic* motivates *Reasoner* to discern and clarify, so that *Reasoner* sometimes takes on the role of judge, which he happily does to maintain his privileged position. *Reasoner* constantly reacts to his frustration with *Victim/Saviour*.

Victim/Saviour's the sleepiest character. He tends to be focused on Sok's internal process. When he joins up with *Hermit*, they indulge in various modes of escapism, preferring to stay together in bed for hours fantasizing and daydreaming. Among this exhaustive gamut of characters, *Hermit*'s the one who knows how to save and replenish Sok's energy. The way he does it is by not going out. This is necessary because given the intensity of *Destroyer/Sabotager* combined with *Warrior*, Sok's vitality levels can rapidly hit rock bottom. However, with the verve gathered through the utter boredom Sok feels from being a *Hermit* and total recluse, *Hedonist* comes along, desiring to use it all for the sake of a good time. When he collaborates with *Destroyer/Sabotager*, everything becomes like a last minute party on the Titanic. This happy festive feeling, generated through their general attitude of there being no tomorrow, is just what *Junkie/Addict*'s been waiting for. Like a hungry zombie, *Junkie/Addict* will never give up on trying to get the feelings back; however, with *Hedonist* on board, he tends to confuse pleasure with feeling. When *Clown* joins in, Sok will consume fast, like an SUV.

Clown comes along when Sok's in public situations, ready to give an unsolicited performance. He does it to save Sok from the embarrassment of feeling awkward in a different culture or when he's saying something inappropriate. *Clown*'s black comedy can sometimes have aggressive undertones, especially when he's with *Skeptic*. But without *Skeptic*, if *Clown*, *Junkie/Addict* and *Hedonist* gang together they have the potential to throw a circus that can totally exhaust Sok. Fortunately, this situation is eventually corrected by *Skeptic* and *Reasoner*, who are usually able to redirect Sok back to his reclusive *Hermit* rehab where he summons up enough energy for his next journey into the circling *framework*.

Sok's satisfied with all his characters, priding himself on how multifaceted he is. He likes to think that the description of the *Rider, on his head are many crowns (12)*, is referring to his own twelve characters. Sok would say the reason he knows about them is because he's the detached, watching and listening, governing body. He understands his characters are his built-in defense mechanism, the result of his propensity to doubt.

Nevertheless, Sok always listens to them and gives them a fair chance to play themselves out, even though almost every time it turns out to be disastrous. Sok would know that more than anybody. But he's also aware that the only way to achieve what he wants is to learn from their mistakes. Invariably, he and his characters will come to see the outcome of their own calamitous performances, each of which Sok has allowed. But through this grinding, precarious process of repeating the same mistakes, he knows they'll learn. In Sok's simple ruling of fairness his verdict is always, *You never know until you try!* Their accumulated, twisted decisions have for the most part been based on their outcries about the injustices of their traumas. They're like inmates who have a lot to say to the world. When Sok gives them chances to make mistakes, they eventually come to see that none of their traumas has been unjust. By maintaining this flexible attitude, Sok's gained self-trust and self-respect by allowing his characters to come and go freely, and easing them away from their need to domineer one another. Sok's characters used to call him King Solomon, and he's considered them to be his council that dwells in his body as he experiences his kingdom living as Sok.

Sok's the first-born and oldest of his characters, the Peter Pan-like inner child who birthed himself into being before any of the traumas. He has twelve offspring, who ironically have always appeared to be older than him, even though they were born later. Over the years, he's learned to divide himself into these characters to cope with the world more effectively. The fact that Sok's now so multifaceted has been the inevitable outcome of his attempts to fit into the world by acting and experimenting through his characters.

Fourth Canvas: **Planet Earth**

Triple Contrast is time travelling! exclaims *Reasoner*, as if he were wiping the steamy surface of a window to *see* through. Upon hearing *Reasoner's* inspiration *Skeptic* sarcastically comments, *When has Sok ever done any time travelling?* Often, *Reasoner* responds. *Can he go back into his former lives then?* *Skeptic* continues. *He should be able to, Reasoner* replies.

In his capacity as *Victim/Saviour*, Sok knows how often he's wanted to revisit his past to correct it. *As if he were watching an old film, how many times has he relived being beaten up by his teachers?* Like a film editor, *Victim/Saviour* watches Sok from the third-person point of view and manipulates the footage into something rather pleasing, while Sok notes that virtually returning the violence to his abusers isn't at all satisfying. *Junkie/Addict* disagrees, thinking this is all the more reason to revisit Sok's past memories oftener.

When Sok was in grade six, his parents decided to transfer him to a richer part of town so that he'd have a better chance of getting into a prestigious junior high school. By then his dad had already gone through a decade of steroid addiction and had failed miserably in his attempts to regain his life after he lost his job with the CIA. It had been a tragic decline, considering how successful he'd been around the time he met Sok's mom, while he was still enjoying a steady rise up the social ladder. At some point, however, after a casual injection recommended by a pharmacist to get rid of back pain, he'd become addicted. Back then no one in Korea knew about the harmful effects of pharmaceuticals, let alone hormone treatments. Over time he became a paranoid asshole who ended up killing himself after being diagnosed with various forms of cancer, the result of a few decades of addiction. All those years, Sok's mom fell into the role of victim, her only thought being that she should never have married him. In reminiscence of their glory days and with no disagreement from Sok's dad, she strived to keep up a wealthy front, dressing Sok and his sister nicely, despite the fact that they often didn't have enough food. Even when they were extremely poor, Sok's dad still kept his hundred ties and twenty suits all custom made by a well-known Korean tailor so that he could continue to look dashing whenever he was in public, along with some secret money so that he could continue to dine alone in nice restaurants.

So looking rather decent, Sok moved to the new school in a wealthier town than the shanty town in which they lived at the end of a bus line. It was a common custom in Korea for parents to bribe teachers regularly in order to give their kids a fair chance at being teacher's pet or at least to prevent them from becoming victims of excessive abuse. Unfortunately, Sok's new teacher didn't receive the customary "thank you money" package from Sok's affluent-looking mom that all teachers expected to receive. The teacher took his disappointment out on Sok, who was already dealing with the pressures of being the new kid that nobody knew in the school on top of being small for his age. At the onset, Sok's teacher beat him in front of the whole class for no reason other than to establish a hierarchy, and Sok had to struggle through.

Somehow he survived, but when he entered high school, again he had to put up with the same family bullshit. His parents enrolled him in one of the most prestigious high schools in Korea. To get to school one way it took him at least an hour by bus. The standard of living in this Seoul town was a hundred times higher than the ghetto apartment where Sok lived. His new friends generally received more money for their monthly allowances than everything his parents owned. He simply couldn't allow himself to have any friends because he was too ashamed to tell them his family didn't have a phone so *how would it even be possible to hook up?* It was even more embarrassing because at that time most other poor families at least had a phone. What made matters worse was that Sok's sister, who was popular and successful in everything she did despite her poor background, made everything seem dignified, as if to accentuate Sok's own fucked-up-ness, like a fresh air reminder.

Unlike Sok who was ashamed of his family's poverty, his sister never hesitated to reveal herself as she was while miraculously receiving respect from her teachers and friends. She was the top student in her school without ever having to study, while Sok, who was forced by his parents to study all the time, was still far from approaching his sister's test scores and grades. Sun was always surrounded with a team of cool, thuggy friends who revered her. As much as Sok loved and respected his sister, as long as she was around he invariably came out the loser. All this, combined with his parent's favouritism, made it easier to go the route of perfecting his *Victim/Saviour* role, all the while neglecting his own empowerment that came from having accepted even harsher traumas than his sister. As a result of holding in his traumas, instead of choosing to let go of his past with his mom and move on to develop himself, he continued to play the *martyr* by being sympathetic towards and always trying to please her. As she'd already perfected her own victim act, subconsciously Sok took his mom on as his role model. At that time he didn't realize his show of compassion was simply a ruse for the pent up anger he felt towards her. Instead he convinced himself that his good will could turn her around. To fulfill his own need, he'd placed himself at his mom's mercy to become the servant of a victim.

Along with the ongoing feigning-he-was-from-a-wealthy-family dilemma, throughout his entire school years, military service and even in a few of the companies where he worked as an adult, he was constantly harassed about his hair. One thing Sok was simply never able to put up with was keeping his hair short. Not only was his long hair practically the only little thing he could call his own to rebel with and hide behind, but also it was a proud Lim clan tradition that all the men, with the exception of Sok's dad, kept their hair long. Everyday of his entire life in Korea was shrouded in the suspense of remaining invisible so that no one would notice his hair. Growing up Sok was appalled that the Korean government prohibited young adult males from having long hair, cracking down on longhaired renegades and legally torturing them in military camps. In his short-lived high school days, whenever there was hair inspection, knowing he'd invariably be sought out, he used to check in voluntarily to the section of the school where the longhaired kids were being held and proceed to tell the teachers in advance that he'd cut his hair. Then he'd rebelliously choose not to do it until the next round. Invariably he was caught and punished.

During the period when Sok was doing his compulsory military service, he devised a way to keep his top hair long in a Mohawk by shaving only the part that was exposed outside his military cap. One day a nasty sergeant, who measured his top hair to be about seven centimeters when it was only supposed to be two max, busted him. He was sent to a correction camp where he was subjugated to the kind of sheer torture the Korean military had been developing for over half a century to fight internal enemies. They yelled at him to plant his head on the ground with his hands behind his back, balancing himself with his toes and the top of his head like a tripod, the typical fare in the military; meanwhile, they either kicked his thighs or left him like that for an eternity. Later when he worked for an ESL school, a branch of a renowned Korean publishing house, he was promoted to be a writer and later a director of the school. Prior to his promotion, he was threatened that if he didn't cut his slightly long hair he wouldn't get the position. Although he told them he'd cut it, he only trimmed it about half an inch and then as if he'd lost all his hair he looked at them straight and gibed, *Now look what you've made me do to my hair!* Through his ingenuity Sok's always managed to keep his hair long, like a cat, always mistrustful of anyone who might be a potential hair harasser. Even though he knew he couldn't beat up his teachers, he maintained his long hair to express his rancour towards Koreans.

When something triggers Sok's memories of his teachers and the associated destructive emotions, he can choose to go into a state of *Triple Contrast* and accept the *feeling*. Adverse emotion in the realm of *Triple Contrast* remains as pure *feeling* without the negative shade of thinking to turn it into emotion, like the immediate physical sensation of a first shot of whiskey. Furthermore, when in the realm of *Triple Contrast*, Sok's prevented from being able to escape from thinking to review in his head the past abuses he's had to put up with. Therefore, *Triple Contrast* allows Sok to remain in the present and experience himself in the first person. This stands in contrast to the emotion-generated memories he has of his past teachers, which normally he perceives from a third-person point of view by colouring or altering them into somewhat satisfying 2D footage, like a movie.

When Sok *sees* his teachers within the realm of *Triple Contrast*, in place of horse images, yet with similar intensity, he *sees* them in 3D appearing before him in first person, as if he's a kid really Kung-Fu-ing imaginary villains after watching Jackie Chan. With the intense *feeling* of the *unknown* to engine 3D realism, Sok's teachers come to life in front of him as a *quantum* image, the more intense the *feeling* the sharper the portrayal. Like a rapid vibration, the high frequency of *Triple Contrast* propels motion to the image as if flipping pages of a cartoon to animate it. Each page is one frame of *Triple Contrast* within a whole cartoon of many frames, ad infinitum. When Sok envisions his teachers in *Triple Contrast*, he's able to relive the experience as if he were really there. Unlike years ago when he was a school kid undergoing the experience of being harassed and escaping into his thoughts to avoid being devastated by his teachers' abuse, now he's learned to relive his traumas in *Triple Contrast* minus the thinking process. The difference is that when his *feeling's* generated within the sphere of the *unknown* in *Triple Contrast*, he *sees* his harassers devoid of the animosity he used to feel, as if it's the first time they've ever met. This relief of being able to return to an original child-like state without feeling resentment is the paradise Sok's always been yearning for and anticipating to happen sometime in the future. Surprisingly, it revisits him from the past at the point in time when his traumas were forming.

To access the *feeling* that allows Sok to actualize his teachers, Sok's decided to use one of his paintings as a visual reference. *Planet Earth* summons the most *feeling* with its 3D focus. During the painting process he set out to carve out the 3D mountains through the angles of the houses. Given the triangular shapes of the roofs, it was challenging to *see* the houses clearly enough to gauge the angles of the rooftops. To paint the houses, as each roof had a different angle depending on where it was situated on the mountain in relation to the viewer, Sok first had to actualize each house in front of him. His repeated use of patterns to delineate his overall image and shapes is his method of creating a 3D perspective, as if each house is a Lego piece stacked up to form a mountain. Later he discovered that his pure *feeling*, engendered through *Triple Contrast*, is the same as *seeing* the world with an equal amount of *feeling* that the painting is generating when viewed in 3D. With that intensity of *feeling* Sok's able to actualize his teachers coming to life just as he *sees* those houses. Next is the painting:

Through this experience Reasoner's learned that innocence is only possible to retrieve in a pure physical state where there's no time perception. Nevertheless, the relived past no longer interests Sok enough for him to continue to engage in it emotionally. It's like the feeling of detachment that comes from the sensation of relief and aloofness he feels after ejaculation. Now from the comfort of his chair, Sok's free to time travel back to the past to retrieve his original childhood innocence that he wishes to apply to the future, only to materialize into the present in *Triple Contrast* with much needed closure and satisfaction. Through time travelling, Sok gets to have digital access to his past memories he's created by grinding himself every day and every second of his life in sequential analogue fashion.

After objectively observing Sok undergoing this experience, *Reasoner* associates it with the image of Buddha in his *Samkyung* lying down on his side with his eyes closed, his hand propping up his head with his mouth widened in a slight grin. He envisages him as dwelling within the realm of *Triple Contrast, feeling* great in his ass while time travelling the universe through his body. That's *Seeing Horses*.

Fifth Canvas: **Snow Over Soccer Field**

S*keptic* poses the question to **Reasoner**: *What if Sok were made to realize that* **Seeing Horses** *wasn't an accident? What if it stemmed from his first child-hood trauma and subsequent cumulative hardships, which just happened to push him towards the unique coincidence of staring at a canvas? Then Sok's life could be viewed as one long chain of piled up accidents caused by his first trauma gone out of control. In that case it might be possible that his poor traumatized self convinced him that* **Seeing Horses** *was the outcome of his believing, while actually it was nothing more than a false pregnancy.*

Reasoner replies that Sok's first trauma and subsequent ones couldn't have been accidents if they were his choice. However, it's true that even after *Seeing Horses*, *Reasoner* was still confused about the difference between reactions and choices, but then resolved the question by reconsidering Sok's dramas with the women in his life, starting with his mom. Sok had some relationships after he separated from his ex-wife, Bari. Although they were enjoyable here and there, mostly Sok was concerned with seeking a trusting human bond. Through his suffocation trauma he'd become a love *Junkie/Addict*, chasing his initial lost bond with his mother through the other women in his life. To really find out whether he could trust someone, *Destroyer/Sabotager* would welcome disasters so that he could observe the quality of the particular person he was involved with at the time. Not only has this tactic never worked for Sok, but also it has always been heavily taxing because it has thrust him to the bottom of his usual bottom.

What Sok usually does with his women is he offers them what he thinks is unconditional love with the one condition that they have to prove they're also capable of unconditional love. So he either waits for a crisis or stages experiments and then scrutinizes their reactions. As if that's not enough, *Destroyer/Sabotager* has the unique ability to stare intensely at a piece of gold until it turns to ash. When he manages to evoke in her an ample amount of emotional reaction, he'll suddenly detach and turn cold. *Reasoner*'s observed Sok's abrupt impersonal detachment causes women to react even more. Then before Sok clearly sees what he's doing, he defiantly pronounces his judgment, thinking privately, *See? Where's the fucking love in her reactions? Why would she react before finding out whether all her traumas were her choice?* Following this, *Victim/Saviour* will make a collective leap to conclude that there's no love on this planet. He'll claim this is due to people's continuous reactions upon reactions based on their original traumas, just as the women in his life have consistently demonstrated.

Immediately after his suffocation episode when Sok observed his mom's stress and misery, he instinctively understood why she'd done it. It was true she'd been thrust into a hard life all of sudden after having grown up with the prospect of marrying well and then initially tasting a bit of success in her marriage. She was beside herself with despair since she'd never learned to accept her hardships so as not to react. Understanding this as a kid after receiving the trauma she'd inflicted on him, Sok vowed he'd do everything he could to protect his mom and make her happy. For a long time, *Victim/Saviour* maintained his belief that he'd made a real choice not to react to the trauma by becoming a murderer, although later on he saw himself as not being any different from his mother.

What Sok was doing with his women was playing his mother's victim role. His courting strategy was that first he offered them paradise and then exposed them to hell to see if they'd be able to accept what he'd inflicted on them, just as he'd received from his mom. However, what he found was that it'd never worked because despite all his efforts, he'd continued to play the role of *Victim/Saviour* as a result of not having fundamentally dealt with his original trauma. It was true he'd had a certain amount of emotional satisfaction in acting like a woman hater. Furthermore, he'd been blind not to see that his decision to serve his mom hadn't been love either. This came clear to him about six months away from finishing his book when he got to say his final farewell to his mom.

The last time Sok saw his mom, they'd finally come to a mutual understanding that it might be the last time they'd ever see each other. A few days later, she phoned him from the airport, as she was about to leave Canada to return to Korea. In her sad voice she whimpered, *If I did wrong in the past, let it go and live well from now on.* Upon hearing her words, Sok felt that in the end there was no difference between them, since they'd both finally come to a mutual understanding that neither of them had been right or wrong. At that moment he realized that love is a willingness to discern the shades of grey within the black and white spectrum.

But the irony is that he was only able to get there through his readiness to withdraw and detach from all his women, family, jobs, social life and dwelling places, each of which at the time could have lured him to stay. Regardless of his multiple personality disorder with each of his characters demanding something different, Sok felt secure in the knowledge that he was willing to let go of everything for the sake of finally gaining clarity as to what making a choice really meant.

The phone call from his mom was a major detachment in his life from which he received the gift of clarity. The call was one of the most profound deaths he'd ever experienced and the deepest love he'd ever felt. In that moment his past memories flashed before him. For the first time, he envisioned he and his mom as two naive kids coping with their harsh realities as best as they could; yet after so many years, they'd come back to where they'd started, both still poor and insecure. With a huge feeling of release, he was able to break his old *framework* and start his new one.

With the prospect of starting a new life, *Reasoner* began working on clarifying the concept of choice for Sok's book. He saw that choice isn't merely a matter of selecting between fries and salad; nor is it a simple calculation of odds based on a consideration of calories or alkalinity or reaction to current needs. Choice means deciding between everything a person *knows* and the *unknown*. Everything Sok *knows* is the gamut of his characters, the collective thinking entity that has access to all his memories, experience, learning and information. As long as his characters are around, making a choice is a matter of cold, selfish calculation and a mere repetition of what Sok already *knows*.

Through this understanding of choice, *Reasoner* was able to see that Sok had made the real choice later in his life of deciding to go for the *unknown*. The *Killer* in him could've convinced him to become a murderer; on the other hand, *Victim/Saviour* might've continued to serve on as a mama's boy, stealing his mom's chance to finish one *framework* as well as Sok's opportunity to become a choice maker. *Reasoner* began to see Sok's past as one long extended reaction to his suffocation trauma. Regardless of whether the process of making a choice takes a second or a million years, in the final analysis it's still a person's choice. Sok's initial trauma was the first stage in his journey to complete the loop, resulting in his choice much later in his life to end the *framework* and begin a new one. In that sense, Sok's first trauma was also his choice, just as now his decision is not to follow the same route as his mother by allowing *Victim/Saviour* to continue to reign over him and his other characters. Nor is his choice to continue in the bloodline of Cain by killing or becoming a mass murderer.

Ultimately his choice has been to let go of his familiar past in favour of embracing the *unknown*. It's *Seeing Horses*.

Next is one of Sok's paintings, *Snow Over Soccer Field*. Its emptiness reflects the coldness and aloneness he's felt throughout his life. At the same time the painting reveals his ability to transform those feelings through *Triple Contrast*, turning his emotional devastation into sadness, beauty and calm. When he looks at the barely visible second goal post located inside the one closer to him, he opens up a 3D space through *Triple Contrast* within which he transmutes his emotions.

Sixth Canvas: **Tongue**

As *Reasoner's* already pointed out, if Sok's initial trauma were his choice there'd be an inevitable consequence. For Sok the outcome was being able to own his new perception that his traumas were his choice. By accepting responsibility for his past, he could detach himself emotionally from his abusers and live free from the traumatized feeling. Therefore, his choice to perceive himself as being trauma-free resulted in his being able to actualize having a trauma-free life. Likewise, if a person perceives of his death as annihilation, that's exactly how he'll experience death when it comes. In his next life or *framework*, he won't remember he died believing and perceiving his death was annihilation. But not realizing his death wasn't annihilation, since he came back with the same old perception he had when he left his former life, he wouldn't have any reason to believe his coming death wouldn't be annihilation, and therefore, would once again perceive it as such, thus playing out the same old *framework* again and again. Here *Skeptic* challenges *Reasoner: Let's say Sok were the only one who didn't view his death as annihilation. For Sok to have physical and decisive evidence concerning his statement, everyone else would have to die first with the same sense of annihilation. But how can he explain it to people if they're all dead?* Although *Reasoner* considers *Seeing Horses* to be sufficient evidence of the existence of a new *framework* as introducing a new perception of life, he explains that the concept of matching a person's perception with the corresponding results is easier to understand.

Reasoner knows that Sok isn't a fortuneteller and can't predict what will happen to someone else, since he has no way of knowing what choices other people will make. However, over the years he couldn't help noticing recurring patterns in people's choices concerning death. In Sok's own life, in addition to his suicide attempt, there've been two major deaths that have held significance: his dad's and his sister's.

Sok's dad was a fan of modern medicine, even though he was generally skeptical of moneymaking scams, which in his mind pretty much
included all other areas of business, pharmaceuticals being his one convenient oversight. Being of the generation of Koreans who understood
they'd been rescued by the Americans twice, first from Japanese colonization and then the Korean War, Sok's dad welcomed most American
products such as Spam and antibiotics because he felt they symbolized
what was modern, effective and innovative. When he was six, Sok remembers the first time his dad brought home a can of Spam. Sok thought it
was the yummiest thing he'd ever tasted. He loved everything about it:
the shape of the can, the attached can-opening device, the meat gel and
its fatty saltiness. Especially since he hardly ever got the chance to eat
any kind of meat, let alone canned meat from the USA, he wished he
could have it everyday instead of only once every few years. Back then
canned food symbolized quality goods. Moreover, since Sok's dad was a
staunch proponent of western medicine, he misinterpreted the relief he
found from his monthly steroid treatments as healing. As a result, he'd
been a steroid addict ever since Sok could remember and remained one
till his dying day. Almost every night, his dad suffered from the grue-
some side effects of the steroids, for which he gradually required more
and more drugs. Sok remembers freezing winter nights being woken
up to walk about forty minutes to a drugstore and back to get his dad's
medicine; at that time, pharmacies didn't require prescriptions.

Soon Sok became the family's errand boy. In addition to nightly
pharmaceutical runs, he also administered his dad's monthly steroid in-
jections. On top of this, since Sok was always grounded after school, he
became his dad's guinea pig for practising acupuncture, which involved
allowing himself to be poked everywhere on his body. Sok wanted his
dad to become a master acupuncturist so he'd be able to cure himself of
his various ailments. Often his dad asked Sok to round up herbs or small
animals known to possess certain medicinal qualities. One time Sok was
given a cat by his friend, pretending that he'd promise to take care of her.
Instead, he brought it home for his dad to boil and consume as medicine,
since for years he'd been listening to his dad's claims that eating a cat
would cure him. Sok really hoped the cat would make his dad well again
so that he wouldn't have to take all that medicine. Although he didn't
actually like his dad much, he was trying to be family. Another time Sok
netted fifty sparrows in a chicken coop that his dad said he wanted to
barbecue. In the end nothing worked, and he was diagnosed with cancer
that eventually spread all over his body. Although steroid addiction was

his dad's choice, Sok couldn't help asking, *Why in the world was such a thing as steroids manufactured in the first place?*

Sok doesn't consider it coincidence that his dad ended up choosing pesticide as his suicide method; at the point his dad's love affair with chemicals and medicines had reached a forte, he'd perfected his role as a victim of chemical dependency. Later on Sok came to the conclusion with regards to modern medicine that there was no difference between healing and hurting. So-called remedial processes seemed to involve interminable pain that never resulting in healing, but rather, just increasing pain. He now sees his dad as a victim who chose to believe in the magical curative powers of western medicine over his own capacity to heal himself, and in so doing, ended up only harming himself further. So in Sok's view, it was fitting that his dad died from a strong brew of pesticide. Ultimately his pharmaceutical drug addiction was a symptom of his dissatisfaction with the present, which impelled him to focus all his energies on finding ways to improve his future. That was what he'd chosen to do with his life.

Although Sok's dad ended up killing himself, the fact that he tried so many ways to stay alive was an indicator that he hadn't really wanted to die. Unlike his dad, Sok really did want to die, which is the reason he's always wondered why his dad had succeeded in killing himself while Sok hadn't. He realizes it was because the two of them had a different relationship with death. What made Sok different from his dad was his childlike curiosity about the *unknown*, though he did follow the family tradition of favouring chemicals such as sleeping pills as his preferred method of dying. Just before taking the pills Sok thought, *If death is annihilation, that's fine, though I'm curious about the **unknown** state I'll go through.* But his experiment didn't work. To really come to fathom the *unknown*, Sok had to come a long way to grasp it through *Seeing Horses*. The expression, *Be careful what you wish for*, is something Sok can relate to, since his one wish to grasp the *unknown* took a long time in coming. But if the outcome of his suicide was to play out his desire to encounter the *unknown* through a brush with death, *why then did his sister, who was ready to accept the **unknown** as she was dying, actually have to die?*

Sok never would've imagined that his remarkable sister could allow herself to become a victim, though on reflection he sees that her imminent fall was already apparent right after her wedding. About a year into her marriage, Sun began to feel pain from a lump in her breast. When she ran it by her husband, whom she trusted as an up-and-coming gynecologist and fertility doctor, he told her it was nothing to worry about and not to bother even getting it checked out. For two years he maintained his expert opinion until finally on her own she felt the need to go have it looked at and was shocked to find out she was in the late stages of breast cancer. Even before her diagnosis, she'd wanted to leave Young, who'd already demonstrated his particularly Korean male quality of putting himself first, priding himself in his superior status as a doctor, man and son of a once well-to-do family. For most Koreans those reasons are more than sufficient to be respected.

As Young represented the epitome of modern medicine, he had everyone's unreserved approval to play with the odds on the lives of his patients and even his wife. On the other hand, as a young person growing up in the same bottomless pit as Sok, Sun'd had ample experience of holding her own; yet as a married woman struggling with cancer and a newborn baby, she just wasn't able to follow her heart and stand independently. On top of that, by leaving her husband Sun didn't want to disappoint her mom who was busy enjoying her enhanced social position of having a doctor son-in-law. Young conveniently took charge of everything, arranging his wife's surgery, radiation and chemo. So just like her dad, Sun fell into the victim role of neglecting the present by depending on her husband, doctors and modern medicine to secure a future she would never get to enjoy. When Sun was in ICU and death was imminent, Young tried certain experimental treatments on her, which only ended up exacerbating her already agonizing death. In the end, like her dad, she died as an experiment of modern medicine.

When Sun was dying in ICU, she took her anger out on Sok for not letting her die, as if he had the ability to perform euthanasia, like Doctor Kabochian. Even before that, she'd been disappointed in him for not being more successful so that she'd be able to depend on him rather than her husband. One day in ICU, Sok told her straight, *Why don't you just die?* and then left. She died within a few days. In retrospect, Sok tried to understand why he'd said what he did, which was so in keeping with the Lim tradition of family betrayal. He realized that over time a person's unfulfilled needs can turn into resentment, as in the case of Sun, who'd never actually gotten to depend on him financially. Therefore, as her best friend, Sok detached himself from her dependency and allowed her the last minute of defiance she needed to pass on.

A few months before her death, quite uncharacteristically, Sun turned to religion. To Sok's surprise, suddenly she was allowing ministers and their wives to come and pray for her. However, after Sok urged her to die, she let go of her dependency on him or anyone else. As a result, a couple of days away from her death, standing alone as she had since birth, when the minister's wife asked her whether she believed in God to prepare her for a Christian passing, she shook her head defiantly. After her death she continued to be Sok's role model.

Sok's dad and sister ended up living dependently, although in Sun's case, she at least let go at the last minute to complete her *framework*. She became the person she'd always been when she was young, accepting the *unknown* and at death returning to it. Nevertheless, even after choosing the *unknown* she still wasn't able to pull out all her tubes and walk out of ICU. Sok sees a person's life choice as being the difference between death and *Seeing Horses* as means of returning to the *unknown*. In his opinion, any choice other than *Seeing Horses*, including Sun's, falls short of being qualified as choosing to be done with the old *framework*. In order for a person to make such a choice, he has to begin by achieving a state of no dependency, which involves letting go of the human tendency to strive for a better tomorrow. When a person stops concerning himself with improving his future predicament, there's no longer a hurting of self by means of medication or stress. To initiate a new beginning, the person has to shift his perception of death as annihilation and alter his attitude of being willing to do anything to prevent it.

On considering Sok's own perspective of his sister's story, *Skeptic* observes that it might make sense to some while not to others. *Reasoner* chimes in that Sok's own personal perception could indeed lack objectivity, so to clarify the issue he discerns that a similar pattern in people's collective fear of environmental disaster can actually lead to potential or perceived annihilation. It's already been established that due to the *unknown-trust cycle*, fear of death is everyone's deepest trauma. This can be applied to the collective trauma of the current environmental crisis. That humanity has decided to perceive the destruction of the planet and human civilization as annihilation is apparent in the global reaction to do anything to prevent the disaster. In fact, *Reasoner's* strategy is to lay out how the very perception of the impending crisis as annihilation will inevitably result in annihilation, whereas the apocalypse[1] is *Seeing Horses*.

In 2011 it's difficult not to notice that environmental change has become imminent and far-reaching. A sharp contrast between the previous natural condition of everlasting glaciers and current rapid glacial melting has become apparent. Like Sok's dad and sister, the planet is dying of

---

[1]Sok understands apocalypse to mean a *lifting of the veil, revelation* or *enlightenment*, an exposure of that which has been hidden from people during an epoch consumed by falsehood and misconception.

cancer from a toxic overdose, so that any interruption in the continuum automatically brings with it a preoccupation with the future. Contemplating this *Reasoner* asks, *What are people going to do if the current rate of melting continues?* He's observed that the future projection of there eventually being no ice, along with its anticipated devastating consequences, has caused the collective global reaction that people are becoming conservationists racing to maintain the current state of the planet. *Skeptic* remarks that the phenomenon is similar to keeping a terminal patient alive indefinitely without making an active decision one way or the other. But really the only way to halt the deterioration would be to revert back to its starting point, like saving falling glass from breaking by holding it firmly in place to keep it from moving. To apply this concept to the case of Sok's dad, this would necessarily entail a return to his natural youthful state before he became chemically dependent. Again *Skeptic* interjects, *But how would someone know a medicine was harmful without first being harmed by it?*

Skeptic also can't help asking: *Would environmentalists still madly be trying to conserve the planet and her species if it meant the extinction of the human race?* He suspects that at the end of the day conserving the environment is humanity's ploy to conserve itself, just as parasites in a person's gut would *Go Green* if the life of their host were threatened. *Reasoner* agrees that the main purpose of conserving the environment is to preserve humanity. From nature's point of view, the only solution would be to eradicate the human population in order to regain a healthy global ecosystem and prevent it from ever being disturbed again. But for the majority of the human population, acknowledging this would be to go against people's efforts to save themselves, ultimately the source of the disturbance. *Wouldn't Sok's dad's efforts to recover his health have been more effective if he'd given up trying to cure himself by increasing his intake of pharmaceuticals on top of the steroids?* Paradoxically, rescuing himself was counterproductive to conserving himself. To paraphrase Nietzsche in *Thus Spoke Zarathustra: Are humans to be overcome by humans themselves?*

What *Reasoner* wants to address is: *How was the continuum broken in the first place?* He returns to the point that destructive human activities originate in a fear of death. Since the death of an individual is inevitable, the human race has desperately been trying to discover immortality with miracle drugs or cloning technologies. Any possibility of defying death has seemed worth trying, even if it breaks the natural equilibrium. But eventually industrial and technological developments have brought what people fear most: personal and collective extinction. This has given them all the more reason to try harder to find the cure for death by painting everything green with toxic paint and melting the ice even faster. However, before reacting to an instinctive fear of death in the name of progress, *wouldn't it have been more intelligent for the human race to probe more deeply into the question of death?* Instead of confronting this fundamental existential question, both individually and collectively, human beings have repeatedly opted for exploiting the planet out of self-interest, not realizing they'd never find the elixir they were looking for. From this viewpoint *Reasoner* recognizes that the inevitable result of living with a fear of death is individual and collective annihilation.

Reasoner's observed that among many areas of human development, science in particular has promoted the understanding that after death the physical body decomposes into different chemical compounds that return to the earth. Just before dying, a person's thinking self believes he'll be gone soon, while strangely the mixture of physical elements that make up his body will continue on. To the thinker, this self-nihilism is perceived as non-existence. *Reasoner* calls that person *T*, the thinking entity. *T* views his life as a one-time deal, regardless of whether or not the planet or universe will continue on without him. Paradoxically, to know the truth about death he has to die, yet at the same time, death is the one thing *T* wants to avoid at all cost. As a result, he diverts his existential crisis by creating ongoing environmental disasters all in the name of progress. *T* is the gamut of Sok's characters, his dad, his sister and the entire Lim clan, all of whose thinking selves have driven them either to extinction or close extinction.

T believes only the physical world exists, whereas the *unknown* is something inconceivable. At some point, however, he knows he'll inevitably confront the *unknown* when he ceases to exist and his body conks out. But if there were such a thing as the realm of the *unknown*, *T* would exist even after his physical death, like the idea of a ghost, though he hasn't been able to find any evidence even after a whole history of exploitative development. *T* thinks his material body and the material world are real, but what he doesn't know is that what makes materials seem real is the contrastive feeling of the immaterial *unknown*. This is inherent to *Triple Contrast*, which would give *T* a 3D perception, if he were open to it. *Reasoner* inquires, *If it weren't for* **Triple Contrast**, *how would T have known his first apple was real? Would it have been possible for him to compare his first experience of seeing an apple with a prior real apple he'd never had?*

Reasoner's also inspired by eastern philosophy and quantum physics. According to Buddha and Nobel Prize winning physicists such as Heisenberg and Bohr, the objective world is an illusion. From this perspective, *T*'s body is also an illusion. According to *quantum* intelligence, there's no material independent of observation. Just as a video game requires a person to view the screen and play the machine, whereas materials such as electrons act on their own as illusive substances like light or waves when not under human observation, those same electrons behave like particles when actually observed. Viewed in this light, reality's a matter of perception. *Reasoner* concurs that the concept of the universe carrying on independently after human extinction is absurd, as if the universe would continue on its own without any life forms. Nevertheless, breaking the continuation of sustainable health on the planet was *T*'s attempt to know whether he could be immortal just as he perceived his bodily substances to be. What he never realized was that the material world was as illusory as him. Accordingly, *T*'s fear that one day he'd no longer belong to the material world was pointless, since according to his concept of what's real the material world already doesn't exist. For *T* to be existent, as he believes himself to be, he and the world can only exist within the realm of the *unknown*; ironically, the *unknown* has to be present for *T* to exist and even come to believe the *unknown* doesn't exist.

Reasoner concludes that *T*'s attitude of needing first to witness the *unknown* before believing in it has put him at an impasse; unfortunately, he acted by developing and destroying the planet, rather than taking pause to ponder the stalemate. It's like Sok's dad whose fear of death and desire to improve his life predicament caused him to experience such excruciating pain that he had to turn to drugs, which eventually required him to take more and more drugs to alleviate the side effects. Or it's like the entire human race that throughout history has been willing to destroy the planet instead of dealing with the void of its own existence, while ignoring mounting side effects such as global warming, pollution and the acidification of the world's oceans. This gambling with the planet, like betting away everything based on speculation, has prevented people from fully considering the crucial question: *What's existence without the unknown? What's sound without silence?*

T's perception that the *unknown* doesn't exist is behind his determination not to make a choice, and ultimately, is what has caused him to become a victim through his perpetual drive towards further progress and advancement. Reflecting on Sok's experience, *Reasoner* can't help but question, *If historically T's been doubtful about everything else, why wouldn't he be doubtful of himself, the one who's been doing all the presumptuous decision-making?* Likewise, *How could Sok's dad not have doubted that his steroids and painkillers were setting his body on fire? And how could he not have doubted that T, his thinking self, was the culprit?* By choosing to let go of his *T*, he could have invited the sense of existence he'd been seeking that would've been possible through *Triple Contrast*. Ultimately *Reasoner* reflects that what Sok's dad needed wasn't immortality, but rather a trust in the *unknown*, which only would've been possible if he'd entered into the *unknown-trust cycle*. If he had learned how to regain his lost trust, *T* could've let go of his incessant searching for cures and answers to the question of his existence. He would've been able to let go of his thinking self and selflessly invited *Triple Contrast*. He would've *Seen Horses*. If the human race had at some point made it a priority to explore and experience that *unknown* state, *T* would never have had to engage in the exploitation of the planet to avoid probing for answers to his existential problems. It's always been *T*'s choice and continues to be. The question now at the end of the world as we know it is whether *T* will be able to let go of his need to conserve himself in order to conserve himself.

Next is one of Sok's paintings, *Tongue*. Sok *sees* the houses as empty shells of the cells of a tongue, the towers as taste buds and the water as saliva. Human beings live as a macrocosm of cells that make up the planet, and the houses they live in are like the shells of cells in the body of the planet, just like the microcosm of cells that live within human bodies, including the tongue. Therefore, human beings are a connector between the macrocosmic and microcosmic worlds. However, in this painting Sok doesn't depict or envision any people in the houses, as if they're the cells of a dead person.

→

Seventh Canvas: **Flow Chart**

1 Three Consecutive Rooms

Skeptic challenges *Reasoner* on the concept of predetermination:

> *According to **Reasoner**, the human condition hinges between feeling lost at birth and fearing the **unknown** at death, unless a person's aim is to regain original trust by **Seeing Horses**. At any given time anyone who believes without a doubt can **See Horses** just like Sok. **Skeptic** imagines that history's mapped out like a video game designed to go on until a person begins to trust through **Seeing Horses**, like the final step in a flow chart. All human activities eventually funnel into that goal of history. In that case, Sok's activity would be predetermined, like travelling on a train track; it wouldn't be an accident, but it also wouldn't be his choice in that it would've been god or someone's. Sok would be a slave who needed an entity or person to lay out a train track for him.*

Even *Reasoner* has had difficulty coming to a clear understanding of predetermination. Later on he grasped that predetermination is a choice that's made in the present. The choice maker's the one who creates the *flow chart* and enters into the new *framework* the moment he makes his choice, so that *Seeing Horses* isn't predetermined by god or something else. Sok's had to go on a long journey to come to this insight.

Growing up Sok mostly hung out with his sister. They'd usually do things on their own, silently and separately, yet in close proximity, taking secret satisfaction in their telepathic communication. Mostly they shared the same intensity of focus. Once when Sok was about four, he and Sun were examining the dazzling sparkly minerals in the dirt of a narrow bridge extending over a creek. Halfway over the bridge, a car came up to them and honked. They were so engrossed in what they were doing that they didn't hear, so the driver assumed they were deaf. Out of concern, he took them home, asking for directions from neighbours along the way. But when he explained the story to their mom, he was perplexed when she told him they weren't hearing impaired.

In the next painting, *Three Consecutive Rooms*, viewers can reflect on Sok's intensity of focus. When he *sees* the three sets of traditional Korean double sliding doors from the initial bunch of brown lines on the canvas, he envisions the 3D space created by the three rooms. Then with an extra thrust of visual intensity he envisages the last set of closed doors with a *feeling* of "Open Sesame":

Another thing Sok and his sister shared were their frequent out-of-body experiences. Again when Sok was around four, he was watching his mom mending clothes while having the sensation of hovering around the room looking down at his own body that would not respond, like it was dead. Suddenly Sok heard his mom thinking as if she were saying to herself, *If I keep sewing they'll think I'm working hard for them.* Later when Sok asked his mom why she'd said that, she got angry. From then on he rarely went out of his body and stopped being able to hear people's inner voices, though he could still hear his own. Looking back, Sok's obsession with human psychology derived from losing this ability and was his attempt to rebuild his way of intuiting people's thoughts. Nevertheless, the fact that Sok and Sun still had an ability to *see* through people continued to isolate them. They always went in cahoots, knowing people were doing and saying things to hide what they were really thinking. They noticed the only people who never lied were their dad and other members of the Lim clan. Following in the Lim family tradition, Sok and Sun almost never told lies either, naively believing their thoughts were just as naked to others. Since their directness and detachment made them different from other kids, they preferred hanging out together.

With his sister as his best friend and role model, Sok used to have more fun playing house than soccer. He followed her wherever she went, listening to and believing everything she said. One day when they were both in elementary school, out of the clear blue she told him, *I heard the next messiah's going to come from Korea and I think it's going to be you.* She offered no further explanation, but Sok thought maybe she'd heard it from some Christian kids at school. Nevertheless, since Sok had always revered Sun at the same time as he felt inferior to her, he was surprised she thought so highly of him. Looking back, Sok's considered how influential that experience has been throughout his life. He's often pondered, *Did my belief I'd be a messiah come from my sister or was she just the messenger of something predetermined?* The destiny option sounded comfortable, yet less fun, while the possibility of deciding it for himself was both unsettling at the same time as it was empowering.

Later on when Sok was a teenager, his dad's astrologer brother-in-law came to visit. By then Sok's dad was well-versed in astrology after years of attempting to figure out how to alter his life. On reading Sok's chart, his dad's brother-in-law said: *You have the chart of a messiah. Your life's going to be difficult, and you'll find it extremely challenging to prevail. But if you don't persist and pull through, you'll continue to have a terrible life until you die.* Sok and his dad didn't think much of it, since according to his dad, Sok didn't even fit into the Lim clan's spirit of revolution let alone appear to be the kind of guy who'd be a messiah. In hindsight Sok also remembers his uncle explaining how predetermination was connected to a person's life choices. Though intrigued, he mostly forgot about his uncle's predictions until after *Seeing Horses.*

When Sok came across the personal significance of *Revelation 19*, he found himself in one of his most down states with no remaining energy to pursue the burden of discovering his identity. At that time he wondered, *What would happen if I jumped off a bridge? If I were actually the **Rider**, wouldn't it be predetermined that I'd survive the fall?* Meanwhile, *Reasoner* was grappling with the enigma of *Revelation 19* having been written long ago when the *Rider's* coming was already predetermined. *Or was Sok just using **Chapter 19** as an excuse to gain whatever clarification he needed?* In the end *Reasoner* decided to treat the problem as if it were a riddle that held the key for Sok to open the door of the box he was in. Although people often refer to the other side of this door as heaven, *Reasoner* calls it the new *framework.* After decoding *Chapter 19, Reasoner* came to an understanding of how Sok invokes it into the present, even though it was written around two thousand years ago.

To unravel the mystery, *Reasoner* first has to assume that everyone's read *Chapter 19* at least once. Anyone can claim hypothetically that he's the *Rider* since all that's required is words: *Out of his mouth comes a sharp sword with which to strike down the nations 18 ... so that you may eat the flesh of kings, generals, and mighty men, of horses and their riders, and the flesh of all people, free and slave, small and great, ... That [h]is name is the Word of God* qualifies him as well as everyone else. The fact that he's the only one who knows himself—*He has a name written on him that no one knows but he himself*—makes it easier to believe in him, since it's a personal matter that doesn't have to do with anyone else, provided he chooses to believe. But the question is how does it take him from *Point A (no one knows but he himself)* to *Point B*, when he separates himself from others only with his words, *so that you may eat the flesh of kings, generals, and mighty men, of horses and their riders, and the flesh of all people, free and slave, small and great ... His name is the Word of God?*

If a person were as interested as Sok in being the *Rider*, he'd inevitably have to ask: *Would it ever work? How many years would it take? Should I quit my day job to pursue it?* On a practical level *of going from **Point A** (the* **unknown**) *to* **Point B** *(being* **known**) *without any miraculous ability such as walking on water, would it be possible to confront others and win the war between the old and new **frameworks** only with my words, even if I were naturally eloquent? How would I do that? Reasoner* explains that if a person decides to work on getting to *Point B*, he does so only because he believes it's possible. *Otherwise why bother?* He might waste his whole life trying. In order to believe it's possible, he has to know that believing works. Yet, there's always that doubt. That's the predicament. The clue to the riddle is initially to become completely lost and enter into the state of having no life purpose. The state of being lost means not having any particular goal in life. Normally, that lost state ends when a person finds something he wants to focus on, a calling or aim such as being a president or movie star. But in this case, finding something can't terminate being lost.

Being completely lost means having no *known* goal, dependency or judgment. Depending on anything, whether it's god, the universe, luck or other people, implies first having an aim in life. Likewise, moral judgment is a symptom of a goal-oriented life perspective because when a person judges someone or something as being either good or bad, he's invariably thinking, *How are they good or bad for me?* Therefore, to be genuinely lost, a person has to be in a state of utter aloneness without any hint of religious sentiment, dependency or judgment. The lost person becomes a stranger with neither hierarchy nor belief system.

By contrast, if Sok had still been lost when he discovered *Chapter 19*, he wouldn't have identified with being the *Rider* because there wouldn't have been any grounds for believing himself to be. This leads to the second clue that the state of being lost has to end magically without finding any particular life goal. Even if Sok had chosen to be the *Rider* because he liked the sound of it, he'd have been disqualified because the state of being lost was terminated through something he found. The only solution to this conundrum was that he had to *allow* whatever it was to be found without attempting to find it. The solution to the riddle was *Seeing Horses*.

In setting himself up to *See Horses* after a life of desperately seeking without knowing what he was looking for, Sok suddenly stopped his pursuit and *allowed* the *unknown* to reveal itself to him. That's when he *saw horses* and immediately realized that believing works. If Sok hadn't *Seen Horses* first before he ran into *Chapter 19*, he wouldn't have known that believing works and wouldn't have taken on the burden of going to *Point B*. After *Seeing Horses*, however, when he ran across *Chapter 19*, it made sense to him that what he'd always wanted would be found.

Reasoner sees that if Sok hadn't made the choice to *See Horses* at this particular moment in history, *Chapter 19* would still be irrelevant today, and no one would know that the present-day *Rider* had always been predetermined, as if it had been written in a *flow chart*. Before Sok had grasped the concept of the *flow chart*, it had already been predetermined as a probability within the old *framework*, but if he'd never made the conscious choice it wouldn't have come into being. *Reasoner* understands that since what's predetermined only comes into being when Sok decides now to make the choice, future predetermination is the result of present resolve. The *flow chart* or *framework* is neither a creation of the past nor the future waiting to be created. It's *nothingness*, and as such, always exists in the present. It's the duration of a person arriving at the moment of understanding.

Reasoner sees that making a choice is like pressing a button. What constitutes predetermination is that the exact determining moment of pressing the button can be a second or a million years. The difference is in the size of the *framework*. In the case of a million years, the choice maker can be confused as to how a million years ago the choice button could've already existed. *Reasoner* understands that the choice maker doesn't depend on someone else to create the button, since until he presses it, the button doesn't exist. Paradoxically, while making the choice is contingent on *T* not being there trying to find something, at the same time, *T*'s the only one who can make the choice of *Seeing Horses*.

2 Snow on the Old City

Skeptic asks *Reasoner*:

> *If there's no distinction between past, present and future, how can Sok conceive of the **Point A** and **Point B** of finishing his book? Even after the timeless experience of **Seeing Horses**, why did he have to continue struggling to get to **Point B**? What's the difference between waiting for the ship to come in and striving towards a future **Point B**?*

Reconciling *Point B* has been such a huge problem that at first Sok had no idea how he was going to pull it off as the *Rider*. For years even after *Seeing Horses* he woke up every morning with the stress of having to do an impossible amount of homework knowing there was a book to write. Barely stifling his desire to throw a tantrum he'd think, *What kind of bullshit is having only my words to face the world? How's it going to work?* Wanting to have special powers instead of just his words to play his messiah role had generally been tricky. *Skeptic*'s often stirred things up with the challenge: *Are you sure you have what it takes to be the next messiah? Reasoner* might've answered, *Yes, because the fact that Sok **saw horses** meant he was at **Point B** already.* Looking back, *Reasoner* sees that Sok's desire to set himself apart has come from a deep-rooted insecurity about who he is: a human being with superhuman ambition. But it took many endeavours and failures to improve himself before he was able to see that. One of those attempts happened a few years after *Seeing Horses*.

In conjunction with *Warrior*, *Victim/Saviour* has always been in denial that Sok's many efforts to improve himself weren't only not working but unnecessary. Sok even remembers frequently giving himself future reminders that those attempts were the result of not accepting the present; nevertheless, as the intensity of his resolution faded, he'd always fall back on the same old patterns because *Victim/Saviour*, backed by *Junkie/Addict*, couldn't help but try yet one more time. Recognizing that as a sign of doubt, Sok knew the only way to rid himself of his uncertainty was just to keep trying, despite his fear of inevitable failure.

At some point Sok felt that in order to finish his book he'd have to get closer to death to be qualified for the role of messiah. With the conviction that he might finally be able to obtain the ability to manifest instantly, he locked himself into another apartment and stopped eating and drinking water altogether. It was one of his most agonizing experiences. In his waking hours he was either writing cookbooks in his head or fantasizing about drinking buckets of icy cola. Eventually he developed an enhanced sensitivity, so that he was even able to re-experience his first real dairy ice cream when he was six as if he were eating it again; he remembered the deep note of vanilla and nutty smell when he peeled off the wrapper and how awestruck he was by the taste, which was like the yummiest mother's milk. Another thing he thought interesting was that he had this welling up of a desire to pray until he asked himself, *To whom?* Sok's desperation seems to have its own imagination.

On a positive note, he became adept at detaching from his thoughts about food and fluids as often and quickly as he could merely to save himself from further misery. After two weeks, Sok was in such a state of agony from hunger and thirst that all his bodily functions, including his brain, were on the verge of shutting down. Then one night when the moon was full, Sok was saved by *Skeptic's* remark: *You need to consider what it is you're really waiting for.* Once again Sok had caught himself being a future seeker, always the same old Sok, unchanged, no matter how hard he tried. The problem was that he just couldn't let go. Over the years, however, he simply got to know better.

Skeptic kept pressing, *Then why hasn't* **Point B**, *Sok's book, happened yet? Is it ever going to be finished?* With such questions droning inside Sok's mind, *Reasoner* often wondered whether Sok had been making the right moves to do absolutely everything he could to finish his book; rather, *mightn't Sok's* **Point B** *best be achieved by dropping everything and keeping his claim to be the* **Rider** *to himself until the day he died?* **Reasoner** now sees that to know the inevitability of getting to *Point B* is to grapple with two contrasting levels of perception: predictability and coincidence.

Before *Seeing Horses* Sok didn't fully trust in the inevitability of living. As life seemed full of random coincidence, he was always calculating how not to fuck things up by choosing something retarded he'd regret later. Eventually those self-generated disappointments began to hinder his belief in the inevitability of the process of living. From that perspective, one wrong choice had the potential to fuck up his entire life. He became confused, thinking it was always a matter of choosing between opposite poles of A or B. Like family trees, choices had the potential to branch off into various possibilities, and on bad days nothing seemed inevitable.

After *Seeing Horses* Sok began to reflect on how events had always been bound to happen and how he should've trusted more in the inevitability of their return to *nothingness*; but at the same time, he saw that such confusion was unavoidable. He started realizing that when facing a choice, the dualism between the option of A and B had to be negated to *allow* what he wanted to manifest in the present, like a time warp. According to *Reasoner*, the ultimate achievement of *Point B-to-be* is happiness, the goal of every human endeavour. Ironically, Sok's own pursuit of feeling whole and happy was what had always kept him unhappily up at night, and could be why others opt for killing or cheating in their desperate attempts to achieve any kind of satisfaction. Now when facing a choice, Sok draws the *feeling* of his future *Point B* into the now, choosing it over a dualistic concept of *A* and *B*. When he does this, he *feels* a blissful physical intensity in *Seeing Horses*, knowing that what he desires is already there in the present. His presencing of *Point B* gives him doubtless calm by *allowing* either *A* or *B* to sort themselves out naturally. In the case of deciding on one road over another, he goes with what he thinks will satisfy his curiosity the most, trusting that what forks into two will inevitably meet again later. There's no such thing as a mistake or regret, and he's free to do whatever he wants.

Regardless of whether Sok fluctuated back and forth wondering what would happen if he dropped out from finishing the book and becoming the *Rider*, his choice had already been made in the intensity of the *feeling* he generated in *Seeing Horses*. What took time for his choice to come to fruition was deliberating on whether or not he should reveal his secret. Even if he decided not to, it would merely be a thinking process that prompted an action that only slowed down the manifestation of *Point B* and would just become another fear-driven mistake. Nevertheless, as Sok's misery increased, eventually he let go of the temptation not to reveal his secret in order to *allow Point B*, the book, to be manifested.

Sok reflects that he used to view *Point B* as a fixed position in time, deluding himself that it would arrive when people finally knew about him. In that state of self-doubt, he had the illusion that he was travelling to *Point B* to become the doubtless *Rider*. For there to be a *Point B*, he thought he had to create a time warp, like pulling the end of the red carpet to the beginning. What he didn't realize was that he was waking himself up more and more frequently to the notion that he was already at *Point B* running onto the red-carpeted treadmill. As he came to acknowledge his pointless struggling to find the right choice based on learning from prior mistakes, he gradually relaxed, which woke him up further to a *feeling* of calm that resembled the sensation of *Point B*. Through this aggravating process, though it was as natural as breathing, and since he didn't yet fully believe in the inevitability of what was happening, he began waking himself up more often. For him to fully awaken to grasp the inevitability of *Point B*, however, he had to travel to what for him was *Point B* in real time because that was when he fully grasped *Point B*'s timelessness.

After hearing Sok's story, *Skeptic* admits to accepting *Reasoner*'s explanation as to why Sok was waiting to acquire uncanny abilities. *On the other hand, why shouldn't it be possible for a person to be able to walk on water?* *Reasoner* responds that it's because people haven't completed their *framework*. Until people separate themselves into two groups, one choosing to go for the new *framework* and the other deciding to continue on with their past ways in their old *framework*, there won't be any uncanny manifestations such as walking on water. It's because *Reasoner* sees the danger of that becoming the sole motivation, which would be no different from the carrot Christianity's been dangling over people's heads with concepts of the miraculous and inevitable such as heaven and hell. Some might spur themselves on only to obtain a certain power over others, rather than genuinely choosing it regardless of the odds. But if certain individuals honestly achieve *Point B* with no exterior motives, inevitably they'll own the magnificent *feeling*. For choice not to diminish into a calculation of odds, the outcome of choosing the *unknown* should always be *unknown*. For the same reason, someone's dead father can't come back to life to free his son from the fear of death because freedom can't be given. It can only be achieved. Otherwise, the freedom-seeker will forever remain a slave to himself, dependent on an illusive promise. According to *Reasoner*, as much as Sok's choice and everyone else's is an individual one, finishing history is a collective event that demands a *framework* that won't accommodate any kind of dependency, which is basically an attitude of waiting or procrastinating on making a new choice.

Next are two of Sok's paintings, *Snow on the Old City* and *Powerlines in Snow*. He's chosen them to simulate the sensation and creation of *Point B*. With their faded look, the paintings invite an attitude of calm acceptance and detachment. *Point B*'s the sensation of the sound of snow.

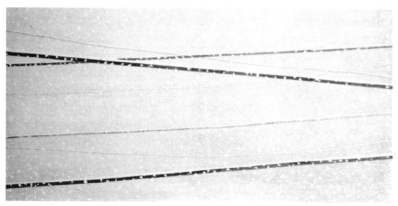

Eighth Canvas: **Markets 1 & 2**

*S*keptic addresses *Reasoner: It was fluke accident that the apple fell on Isaac Newton because it wasn't his choice. Even so, he was able to bring a new perception to humanity without having to make the choice of believing.*

Sok's always been fascinated by historical icons such as Isaac Newton, or in modern times the inventor of Velcro, George de Mestral, who investigated cockleburs (devil's claw) that clung to his dog and socks after returning home from a hiking trip. He responded to new information differently from how people normally would. Usually devil's claw is considered to be bad luck, as its name testifies, but when de Mestral encountered it, he experienced a gap between the *known* and the *unknown* (what became Velcro later) because he was curious about the plant's microscopic structure, and that's how Velcro was conceived. But Sok's noticed that other than exceptions like Newton and de Mestral, people's decisions are based on what's *known*, like being in a self-limiting box where there's little chance of discovering anything new. Sok's found this to be most apparent in education.

While he was living in Canada, Sok went travelling through Mexico with Bari. At a zoo in Mexico City he overheard an overly zealous mother asking her son what colours the tigers were. In a split second the son blurted out, *Orange, black and white!* Sok was astounded that even at the inquisitive age of five the boy missed the chance to *see* the tiger's multiple shades and colours in *Triple Contrast.* Thanks to his eager mom, his education meant repeating what he knew already. On the flight back to Canada, a woman was sitting next to Sok and Bari. When Sok spoke to her and they exchanged names, he couldn't clearly make hers out above the jet noise. When she said it again he still didn't get it, readying himself to really focus the next time she repeated it. But instead she said her name was *M plus Earl*, like the restaurant chain. Sok got it immediately, feeling instant relief from his stomach tension. Afterwards, he realized how easy it is to stay within the realm of the *known* based on what's familiar, like *M plus Earl*, and how much more effort it takes to hear in *Triple Contrast* the way babies learn languages. Sok associates this mode of *seeing* a tiger or catching a name through learned memory with the kind of education that produces dull-mindedness. If the *known* were something fixed, cave dwellers would've been able to get *M plus Earl* from Merle. When it comes to feeling fucked over by education, Sok and the Mexican boy in the zoo are no exception.

All his adult life Sok's faced an impossible struggle to undo what he learned growing up back in Korea. After being taught English in the Korean school system, some of the side effects were certain fossilized habits he couldn't get rid of. Over several years of public school education, he learned from teachers who pronounced English according to *known* Korean standards. Not only were they incapable of comprehending native English speakers, but there was also no way those native speakers would've been able to understand the English the Korean teachers were speaking. Their educational efforts effaced the fact that the purpose of learning language was to communicate. Sok reflects he should've dropped out of school sooner. Growing up, he used to hear Koreans say that unless a person went to live in a western country when he was a kid he'd never learn English. But Sok did because he had to.

In his early twenties, Sok spent many hours a day viewing the *American Forces Television Network* available in Korea. At first he was unable to understand the talk shows but was curious about what could be so funny that it would cause entire studio audiences to keel over with laughter. He was dying to know about something so *unknown* to him. A few years later, his endless TV watching paid off big time when he landed a fantastic job as an ESL teacher in a well-respected company working with teachers from western countries. Since the foreign women seemed to be all about what Sok didn't *know*, he started dating them. But actually this physical attraction to people of different races had dawned on him much earlier when he was around ten. Once a year during Christmas holidays, the Korean Television Broadcasting Station would air western music videos, which were generally prohibited because they were frowned on for being a bad influence. That day Sok felt as if he'd just broken out of jail, though afterwards he was starved to have more. In one video a British group, the *Nolans* (the equivalent of the *Spice Girls* back then), came on singing "Sexy Music," wiggling their superimposed bums in synchronization. This unfamiliar sight filled Sok with a yearning so intense that he felt a pang in his chest.

Going through puberty, Sok wasn't so thrilled with the scrawny, fashion model boyish body type of Korean women, which for him was the epitome of what he already *knew*. As a result, in his sexual fantasies women's bums got fatter over time. Sok's wondered sometimes to what extent his sexual drive has influenced his path of learning English, coming to Canada and desiring to write in English. He knows he'd never have been able to write his book in Korean due to the limitations of the Korean language. Once during his fantasizing days he was looking at a magazine that featured photos of a Canadian marching band with all the women holding up one leg like a goose. In his mind they all appeared to have huge thighs, and Sok knew right then and there that he'd have to go to Canada to see for himself what he didn't *know* in the form of gargantuan asses and enormous thighs.

Looking back, Sok can sum up his life-journey as striving to define what's *known* and what isn't *known*. Since inevitably over time what isn't *known* becomes what's *known*, Sok came to wonder about what the ultimate *unknown* would be. *Reasoner* claims that's the difference between Sok and Newton.

Sok accepts that from Newton's perspective the falling apple was an accident, even though he chose to go for what was as yet *unknown* (in this case, gravity). If Newton hadn't interpreted the falling apple as an accident, his question might've been, *How did I do that?* instead of *What force made it fall?* It's true he chose to go for the *unknown* by creating a gap between the concept of gravity and conventional explanations such as god's punishment, bad luck or the wind. However, while Newton was able to grasp the as yet *unknown* concept of gravity, he was blind to the possibility that it was the result of his choosing the *unknown* by letting go of the thinker, *T*, who invariably goes for what's *known*. However, even after choosing to negate currently held preconceptions by asking, *What **unknown** force made it fall?* he ended up contradicting himself by not inquiring into the more pertinent issue of who was behind the question, *What **unknown** force made it fall?* He was blind to the notion that as long as he assumed the incident couldn't have come from his choice of the *unknown* and eliminated prematurely the possibility that it could've been the result of his work, he was still operating within the realm of the *known* with a preconception as to that possibility.

Reasoner postulates that Newton's self-contradiction exemplifies the majority of people who've accepted the notion of coincidence. The assumption that something's coincidence disempowers the will of two objects to interact, in this case, Newton's head and the apple randomly colliding in time and space as two lifeless specs of dust bouncing towards each other. From Newton's perspective, this accidental collision gave him the insight of gravity, which he concluded was the result of chance happening. Since in his view the random occurrence of the apple falling on his head had nothing to do with him, like stepping on a random turd, at that time he wasn't able to perceive the second collision observed by *Reasoner*. The second collision was between the first collision of the apple and Newton's head on one hand, and his own perception of gravity on the other. If the first collision was an accident of two colliding objects neither having a will nor being willed, it's like saying the second collision between the first one as the physical impact on his head and his perception was an accident as well. In order to maintain the consistency of this unformulated view of the accident for the second collision, his concept of gravity should already have been in his head to collide with the impact of the first collision. It's the same idea as needing two hands to clap. *Reasoner* reflects that in the event of a groundbreaking concept such as gravity, for it to have been an accident, it had to be known before the collision so that Newton would already have it in his head. If so, *From whom did Newton steal the idea?* It might be argued that accidents are limited only to the physical world. But in that case, *How would anyone explain the Placebo Effect, the idea that a person's belief can influence the material world, as in the case of physical healing?* *Reasoner* suggests that the incident of the apple happened to Newton precisely because he already had an inclination towards being dissatisfied with conventional views of what was *known*. *Was Newton's longing for a more satisfying explanation about certain world phenomenon what caused him to create the incident for himself?*

Reasoner reflects that if two cars were involved in a minor bumper-to-bumper accident caused by lightening, and in a rage one of the drivers killed the other, *could the killer argue that his action was also an accident brought on by the initial collision?* Just as in a court of law the judge would say, *No, it was your choice, and we'll gas you,* Newton also actively chose a new concept over a conventional idea. This suggests that accident isn't necessarily coincidental. It follows that every seemingly accidental occurrence opens up *choices*, meaning that accidents are integral to *choice*. *Reasoner* applies the same reasoning to history: *If history were viewed as a series of accidents, and at the last second the lump sum of all those accidents led to a choice of final action, then has the whole of history been an accident or choice?* Choice, *Reasoner* answers because he now understands that if every accident leads to a choice then simply there are no more accidents. To *see* this is to enter into the realm of *Seeing Horses*.

Although *Skeptic*'s question has been sufficiently met, *Reasoner* sees the merit in further examining the possibilities that could've been open to Newton. When it comes to hiding out within the sphere of what's *known*, Sok's found Koreans to be exemplary. For example, out of their fear of the *unknown*, they tend to promote nationalistic values such as *Koreans don't do this or that* as their final argument for just about everything. This has frustrated Sok throughout his life, especially considering the fact that their narrow conception of what's *known* has never been acceptable to him. Their fear of the *unknown* is well-reflected in their embracing of Christianity. When the first missionaries came to Korea, they were given the cold shoulder since what they were peddling wasn't *known* at the time. However, over the years Koreans became comfortable with Christian doctrine and got sucked in by the allure of being able to depend on one God so they'd never again have to worry about an *unknown* future, and because it supported their basic predisposition towards non-action. Nowadays, the spread of Christianity has been so pervasive that one Korean out of two is capable of breaking into tongues at any second, and thousands of Koreans in church can create a mumbling uproar equal to a fanatical army of retards. By now, Christians have infiltrated every facet of Korean society and have even infested government to the extent that with their superior moral ground they've gone in cahoots over non-Christians.

Having lived in Korea till he was almost thirty and obtained his college degree in a theological seminary, Sok's observed that being Christian basically means allowing oneself to surrender to the fate of being controlled by God. Korean Christians like to manipulate other people's lives in order to get the reverse satisfaction of practising fascism with the indisputable moral backing and unlimited authority of God. Rivaling even the zeal of Jehovah Witnesses, their dedication to converting others can be utterly aggressive. When Sok was around twenty-five, he had a Korean girlfriend whose mom was a frenetic Christian. She demanded he spend the weekends attending church with her as a condition of going out with her daughter. After two years of failing to convert Sok, she gave up on him and proceeded to prevent her daughter from seeing him. It was around the time that he landed his job as an ESL teacher. He told his girlfriend that she had to choose between him or her mother. She chose her mother, whose dominance was rivaled only by God himself.

The pervasiveness of Korean Christianity is indirectly documented in two of Sok's paintings of typical modern markets in Seoul, *Markets 1 & 2*. The buildings are vertical markets replacing the old-fashioned horizontal ones. The colours of the various signs screaming out from the buildings stand in contrast to the overall beige starkness of Korea and are a contemporary version of the competing voices of sellers in the traditional street markets that the buildings have gradually replaced. In these contemporary selling places, business establishments blend with churches and clinics with their crosses tinting the glass walls. Next are the paintings:

Not only did Sok despise the invasiveness of Christianity in Korea, but he also hated to talk to Korean Christians since it was difficult to reason with someone who argued that everything was God's will without having any way to prove it. Ultimately Sok doesn't ever like to lose a debate; on that note, *Reasoner* proposes returning to the discussion about Newton.

Reasoner imagines that based on the historical milieu in which he lived, Newton formed a perception that the falling apple wasn't a coincidence.

According to the conventions of the time, when the apple fell on Newton, it would've had to be explained by means of what was *known*, namely, that it was an act of God for it not to be a coincidence. Viewed in that light, the incident comes to be interpreted as either a punishment or gift. But even from such a divided viewpoint, Newton's still the choice-maker (even though he's unaware that he is) and God's merely his servant. On the other hand, in order to dodge the responsibility of making choices and accepting the consequences, Newton very likely muffled his doubts and conformed to popular opinion that the falling apple was God's will to test him by making it appear that Newton was making his own choice. If Newton were a Korean Christian, he'd cry out, *Dear God, it's always been your choice, my Lord!* Even if he had doubts about this, he'd reason that those were also the words of God. He could even kill and still argue that it was God's will, and if he were hated and persecuted, it would still be God's will, and he wouldn't lose his faith. From this common perspective, he could be completely self-righteous without even feeling the need to prove how everything was God's will, since ultimately it's God's will that nobody should ever have to explain how they came to their religious perception.

This time *Reasoner* sets up a hypothetical situation in which Newton chooses to go for the *unknown*, thinking that's also God's will. Entering the realm of the *unknown*, which necessarily excludes *T*, Newton, the thinking entity who thought his choice to go for the *unknown* was God's will, is no longer there. *If the person who chose to think everything was God's will no longer existed at that point in time, then who would've been there to make the choice of convincing himself that at that moment it was God's will? T* would've had to be there in his place. As it's *T* who creates the illusion the notion of God depends on, it's the choice of Christians to continue to pretend to see what they don't actually *see*, as if they're the emperor and the crowd in *The Emperor's New Clothes*, who maintained the consensual hallucination that the naked emperor was wearing a beautiful outfit.

Ninth Canvas: **Shanty Town 1**

*S*keptic addresses *Reasoner* about his concern: *Even if a person wanted to live in the present, he'd never be able to achieve that state, since practically, how could he abandon his life goals and stop waiting for the future? On top of that, the very desire not to have wishes becomes just one more wish to deal with.* Having found that consistently not having any wishes was difficult even after *Seeing Horses*, Sok often reminded himself, *Do I want to get even more fucked up by having more wishes?*

Even though Sok's sister was about three years older than him, growing up they enjoyed the same black humour they felt could only be shared with their dad. One day the three of them were watching TV about an annual monsoon flood along the Han River that cuts Seoul in half. Whenever disaster hit, Sok's family would immediately slip into party mode. That time Sok's mom was making savory seafood pancakes with spicy dipping sauce (*buchingae*), the family's version of popcorn. On that particular year, the river rose up so high that it was only a few feet from sweeping away some bridges. In the middle of a news broadcast emphasizing the need to slow down the rise in water level, their dad blurted out, *Don't you just want to see the damned bridge being swept away?* On that day, Sok and Sun were proud to be members of the Lim clan, a minority of Koreans who found the status quo so unbearable that nothing would suffice, short of a revolution or miracle. Yet the kind of future they desired seemed far away. Feeling the same as their dad about their predicament, they wanted to add: *Yeah, and when's nature going to sweep away the bridges, school and school records, along with all the adults?*

While attending various schools, Sok and Sun often wished there'd be a war so they wouldn't have to go through another competitive, memory-based test at school. If it wasn't going to be a flood, then war seemed to be an equally viable alternative to getting rid of the schools and all their evaluations. In the Korean school system, exams have always been paramount in determining whether students will be able to pass the final rote memory-based university entrance examination that ultimately determines their permanent position in the Korean hierarchy. Still today, it isn't uncommon for certain ten-year-old nerds to be studying till midnight every night under constant parental surveillance. Sok's always hated memorizing, and no matter how hard he tried he wasn't able to bypass those tests. He couldn't imagine his life getting any worse than it already was with the interminable assessment and subsequent harassment from parents about test scores. Some parents would even beat up their kid for being second best instead of first out of a class of seventy. Sok didn't buy any of the sugarcoated promises that grownups would issue out about tests leading to a successful future, and he simply couldn't think of a solution short of war to end all the madness.

When Sok and his sister were in their twenties, Sun met Young, who was at that time attending medical school. From the beginning of Sun's marriage and throughout her struggle with cancer, she supported his internship and residency with her tutoring. Both she and Sok hated tutoring all the time, after spending so many years working to support their parents who kept fucking things up. But they'd never been able to say no to taking on the family's financial burden. Then at some point, their dad showed up with cancer and no money left after having disappeared for several years with a portion of the Lim family inheritance he'd weaseled out of Sok's second uncle and then squandered. Even though by then, Sok and Sun weren't that thrilled to see him, they couldn't refuse him the money he needed for the four surgeries he ended up having. For years, they'd felt torn between sympathy and disgust, but as the situation worsened they couldn't understand why their dad, whose body was riddled with cancer, didn't just decide to end his life. They didn't have the heart to tell their mom to get lost either, even when she repeatedly blew off all the money Sok and his sister had saved, frittering it away on the boyfriends she had during her husband's absences and after his death.

All this was happening around the time Sun married Young. At a certain point early on in their marriage, Sun gave up trying to get Young to stop smoking in the house with her and baby Sang. Furthermore, every night Young would devour two entire meals and drink until he was plastered while watching TV till three in the morning. No matter how Sun pleaded or yelled at him he never stopped, the result being that about ten years later Sun died of lung cancer that had metastasized from her breast.

Throughout the duration of Sun's cancer struggle, Sok continued to live in the future with many desires weighing him down because he felt as long as she was dying, being in the present simply wasn't possible. While living in Canada he was constantly thinking about ways of transforming his sister's future. He even remembers fantasizing about buying a mini-van to make her annual ten-day family visits more comfortable. Around that time Sok had encouraged Sun to become a vegetarian, which she remained until her dying day. In fact, she became so adamant about it that after her death, Sok lamented all her favourite meat dishes she'd missed. While she was alive, he used to entertain hundreds of wishes for his sister, *But where did they belong after her death?* He saw that every-thing would just turn to regret, and that he'd be left with a bag of gold as the last person on earth.

Before Sun's death, one of Sok's future wishes was to become a kid again, free to play with no worries, adult responsibility or impossible work-load. He always felt he'd missed having a proper childhood. Hating to be interrupted by the sound of the school bell, he decided to recreate his own playground with his painting, one in which he was in control and with-out time disruptions. But as he got older, he always felt he didn't have enough money or resources to really play the way he wanted. On top of everything, there was the unavoidable problem that he'd become too old to play in the childlike ways he desired. He didn't realize then that regard-less of his age, today was still the youngest he'd ever be! It was only after his sister died that he was finally able to have done with waiting for his life to begin and face his reality without always wishing for it to be some-thing other than it was. So after Sun's death, without his sister around to impose any more of her dying wishes on him, Sok began to enjoy the vibrancy of his life again, something he'd forgotten.

Next is Sok's first painting after his decision to be a painter. It reminds him of his childhood drawings and paintings of where he used to live. Instead of waiting for his childhood to return to him, he became his child-hood self and simply painted for the sake of painting. *Shanty Town 1:*

In his past readings, *Reasoner* noticed a similar sense of relief in *Plague* by Albert Camus. After losing more than half the population to the Black Plague, the remaining people in the affected area accept their deaths with no hope of a future and begin living in the present, eating every meal as if it's their last, swimming under the moonlight and confessing their love. With the lifting of the heavy emotional impact surrounding the inevitability of their death, they're left to make the most intelligent decision within the *framework* of the plague. Sok believes this level of astuteness only comes after some kind of encounter with death. *Reasoner* fathoms that the collective *framework* of history is like taking a ride on the Titanic.

If a person on the Titanic knew about the impending disaster beforehand, it'd be hard to imagine him opting to work on improving the ship's interior decoration in favour of throwing one last party. *Reasoner* knows that whatever choice that person makes, when the Titanic actually starts sinking, and he knows he has only ten seconds to live, instead of setting his hopes on rescue, he should probably just relax and enjoy being himself in his body one last time, since there's nothing better to do. That attitude of saying, *Fuck it!* is what invites *Triple Contrast*. But to make such an intelligent decision to let go of all future hope, first the person actually has to realize he's on the Titanic. Today everyone's on the Titanic. *Reasoner* understands that to comprehend that is to know the *framework*.

In order for humanity to grasp it's on the Titanic with no hope of rescue, everyone has to chip in with their wishes; all humanity's desires combined into one would be the wish of not having any more wishes. Humanity's last wish should be the final freedom from wishing. Regardless of impending death or extinction, having no more wishes is the equivalent to a person living his dream. If everyone's future wishes circle back to the past, to *Revelation 19*, Sok's claim to doom everyone negates the accumulation of wishes throughout history so that humanity can finally realize it's on the Titanic.

Reasoner understands that feeling the freedom from the pressure of the *framework*, which within the context of the history of humanity is the same as being on the Titanic, is like riding the surf with an incredible sense of abandon. It's like overcoming the unsettling experience of birth that with time grows into dependency or reaction based on an absence of trust. It's accepting the *feeling* of the *unknown*, everyone's worst nightmare. However, now that Sok's in full acceptance of the *unknown*, there are no more worst-case scenarios he feels the need to engage in emotionally. Without emotion blinding his intelligence, he simply makes the best choice within the given circumstances without waiting for anything else he thinks he needs. This is the state of not having any more wishes. It's *Seeing Horses*.

Having no more wishes is being in a state of detachment, not to be confused with showing an uncaring or aloof attitude of indifference. Detachment is a pure blank *feeling* of acceptance or love, free of judgment or emotional engagement. It's the difference between acting cool and being cool. Detachment is:

No hopes.
No saying nice things to others for gain.
No liking someone else's body over one's own.
No saying I love, World Peace or Green.
No striving to save the planet.
No speeches before action.
No keening over the past.
No choking one's desire to say what one feels.
No apologies.
No avoiding being the only asshole.
No bowing to gods.
No tomorrow.

PART 2

Time to reap ...

Tenth Canvas: **Vertigo**

Sok's had the worst sleepy habits. *Victim/Saviour* loves to daydream, so much so that in his mid-thirties Sok started painting intensively in an attempt to wake himself up from the fantasy world he'd developed over the years. In addition to painting, which helped him stay in the present, he continued to put an enormous amount of effort into preparing his meals, cutting his own hair (learning from trial and error how to achieve the exact shape he wanted) and altering his own clothes to make them interesting. He would have been fine, totally self-sufficient, if he had been stranded on a deserted island making everything from scratch. That was one of Sok's childhood dreams, along with becoming a lighthouse keeper. He felt that if he were able to live in such a secluded place, he'd no longer have to dream. However, since he almost always lived in the city, he sometimes went for walks in the mountains at night to feel a sense of being alone and in the present. Regardless of his endeavours to keep himself awake, during these periods *Hedonist* complained about missing out on the things that gave him pleasure and often convinced Sok to settle for virtual alternatives, while *Victim/Saviour* missed fantasizing in his favourite place, his bed.

Sok's numerous sexual fantasies revolved around recurring plots to provide him with certain pleasures he wasn't getting in reality, like a vitamin deficiency. His fantasies were pretty much variations of the first one he had when he was around ten, which at that time hadn't yet developed into anything sexual. The setting was the Lim clan residence where Sok, his mom and sister stayed, and where his mom started suffocating him. In his fantasy, his second uncle, wife and son, his second uncle's mistress and her daughter from Bong Hun, and Sok's paternal grandmother were all watching him show off in some kind of superhero persona. His message to them was: *You've had all the chances in the world to be nice to us, but now it's too late!* Subconsciously he harboured a hidden desire to continue the Lim clan's war, this time making it successful because he was in charge. In his mind, this involved a hero fighting bad guys who were attacking the Lim family residence. *Reasoner's* observed that Sok's later sexual fantasies developed around a similar theme.

Sok imagined having sex publicly in front of everyday Koreans, including children and old people, all shocked spectators opening their mouths and eyes like the woman in Edvard Munch's *Scream*. He chose public places that suited the particular mood, and he liked to imagine doing it in doggie style because he thought it was the most vulgar. His fantasy women had exaggerated womanly shapes. Although he started out employing brunettes as his preference, over the years he became attracted to Caucasian blondes, one of the reasons being that they looked as far as possible from Koreans and the other that he'd been brainwashed by the media. When filling in the details, he'd draw out scenarios that would allow him to get his message across in a way that Koreans would simply have to take whatever Sok did, like a checkmate. On a deeper level, he dreamed of being a role model for uptight Koreans to loosen up and change. He imagined the shock effect of his fantasy spectacles instantly liberating them from all their bullshit.

Due to Sok's special ability to focus in *Triple Contrast* and his years of work developing his kundalini, his habit of masturbating gradually became too real and pleasurable for him to let it go. The hours he spent in bed escaping reality through his daydreams were what eventually led him to realize the limitations of his fantasizing because there wasn't a fantasy satisfying enough for him to stop fantasizing. Eventually he gained a certain detachment from his illusory world and came to discern the relationship between his fantasies and his traumas.

After receiving the trauma of childhood physical abuse, Sok gradually learned how to internalize it as his wish-to-be, like an upside-down image reflected inside a pinhole camera. His desire was the opposite of his receptive self, the imaginary *Point B* of his future emotional compensation. To comfort himself that he'd someday neutralize the trauma, he'd concoct a fantastic vision such as becoming a dark saviour who'd doom the world. Such fantastical projections were *T*'s effort to calm himself down with future images of awesome solutions to having just lost his house, for instance. But since he never had any opportunity to satisfy his desires in reality, Sok didn't see any reason to let go of his fantasizing, the counterpart of his traumas. As long as certain traumas hadn't been dealt with, there'd always be fantasies.

Sok reacted to traumas either externally or internally to make his wishes come true. He reacted outwardly through his competitiveness to get what he wanted, while his internal reaction was depression, his latent desire that found expression through his daydreams. Sometimes he responded through passive-aggression, which in his case had the potential to become full-blown external action. *Reasoner*'s observed that people's inward reactions are collectively mirrored in the common ground of the internet, movies, commercial products, games, financial markets, porn sites, gambling and shocking or funny scenes on YouTube. As on the internet people don't feel they're in danger of losing face, they're more likely to be straight about what they're really after.

After failing to have their wishes come true, people react either by pursuing partial fulfillment through eating, shopping, gossiping and addictions, or only virtually actualizing their desires through movies, television, games, the internet, magazines, thinking and daydreams. Nowadays people occupy themselves with such escapism or virtual realities to find instant gratification while waiting for their fantasies to come true some day in real life. Considering humanity's sex drive, *Reasoner*'s often been puzzled as to why popular demand for video games as a means of virtual fulfillment has failed to explain the sluggish development of virtual reality sex. *Hedonist*'s often thought that video games, movies, porn, sex toys, 3D vision goggles, the internet, real-life robotic dolls, technology for the five senses and chemical mood enhancers should be funnelled into one slick machine. He can't imagine anyone not wanting one if it were as real as reality with slick programs people could guiltlessly choose.

Reasoner knows that what defines virtual reality is its quality of realism that's not quite as real as what a person knows as reality. Among the entertainment choices, some video games invite first person involvement, making things seem more realistic than third-person virtual experiences such as television or movies, despite their still limited visual quality compared to reality. Movies have better visual quality, but since they're experienced in third-person, Sok found he had to replay them as extended fantasies (such as fighting in a medieval battle) to experience what he'd never be able to achieve through his outward reactions. *Reasoner*'s observed that all these virtual attempts turn into non-feeling-based thought process and break *Triple Contrast*. As such media never produce the visceral intensity necessary to generate *Triple Contrast*, they end up offering only partial fulfillment, like daydreaming. In fact, if these virtual experiences actually provided total satisfaction, people wouldn't feel the need to continue entertaining their hidden desires and fantasies.

Sok's most contented state was when he was a kid and still capable of making his wishes come true. He was able to be anything he wanted, such as Batman running around in a cape *feeling* real from being centered in his body. Unfortunately this ability of kids lasts only until enough peer and adult pressure has accumulated to invalidate it. Growing up like everyone else under the bombardment of television and the influx of information, Sok reacted by developing an appetite for plots and fictional characters like those on TV. At first the characters he adopted were his future wannabe's, but as time went on, the images became distanced from his real self. Sok remembers girls back in Korea who were in love with Japanese comic book characters with saucer-shaped eyes and hair for ten people, the Asian exaggeration of westerners. Fascinated by watching the stream of superheroes like the *Six Million Dollar Man* and *Wonder Woman*, Sok grew up feeling that being Asian was an irreversible shortcoming, a sentiment shared by most Koreans.

By the time Sok was ten years old, he was already on input overload and no longer able to play out his wannabe scenarios in first person. Fueled by physical inhibitions that chained him to his school desk, he became too self-conscious to continue his child play. Instead, he switched to fantasizing, losing the *feeling* of being in the present and breaking *Triple Contrast. Reasoner* now sees that Sok's vivid memory of the first time he started fantasizing about acting out in front of Lim family members was because the Lim residence was where the suffocation incidents had occurred. Experiencing the level of satisfaction he achieved through those fantasizations with their temporary mood elevation, he became immediately addicted. From then on, his subconscious mind repeatedly handed him the same script and location, even though Sok didn't consciously think about the Lim residence much after he left. As he continued to fabricate action characters of himself, he began thought-travelling towards a future of someday actually being able to carry out his fantasies and gain the emotional satisfaction of finally getting back at his harassers. In order to pursue such trauma-based desires through his fantasies, he gradually left behind his inner actor, cape and dagger, and further broke *Triple Contrast.*

As a teenager Sok became miserable and defeated as the distance widened between what he wished for himself and his realization of the limitations of what was possible. As he no longer lived in the innocent state of being able to impersonate, like many teenagers he felt utterly unsexy. At that time, he wanted to become a member of Duran Duran, but for that to happen it seemed he'd at least have to be reborn in England. *Reasoner's* observed that Sok and other people pursue sexiness through their jobs, fashion, plastic surgery, working out and addictions. All are attempts to bring those lost feelings back. *Reasoner's* always known that Sok would only really be able to find personal contentment and fulfillment of his sexual desires in a meaningful relationship. He reflects that in his involvement with women, the more thinking and fantasizing he does during a relationship, the lower the level of compatibility and intellectual, emotional and sexual satisfaction he experiences.

When Sok looks back, his women weren't unenjoyable. The main problem was that he hadn't been fully there to appreciate them. He invariably found something lacking in the woman that would minimize his own personal or sexual pleasure and cause him to seek within the virtual realms of the media and his own fantasies what he felt was missing in the relationship. As he'd become chronically incapable of awakening himself often enough from his *T*, real sex had come to feel as disconnected as virtual gratification. Sok had learned only too well how to lock into his own thought bubbles in which he fantasized about fulfilling certain presently lacking aspects in other people and relationships. But *Believer* would always counteract this with the conviction that if Sok were able to find the right soul mate, he might be able to achieve a state of no thought so that he'd no longer feel the need to dwell on her imperfections. With that feeling of inevitability that he just knew would come with finding a destined companion with whom he could have a meaningful friendship and sex life, there'd no longer be the need for conditions or doubts. On the other hand, based on his suffocation trauma, Sok still held to his basic condition that the woman of his dreams would finally offer him unconditional love. He imagined that if he had that, he'd no longer have reason for insecurity or react to the anticipation of criticism. Sok's most important condition was that the unconditional love he was seeking involved no conflict of interest, something he'd never experienced from his parents.

A conflict of interest can be defined as a situation in which a disagreement arises between people as to each other's wishes. Sok often ran into a conflict of interest by placing a condition on the woman in his life that she gave him unconditional love. After enforcing this condition, he screened for the perfect partner with whom he could love and be loved unconditionally, and then he wondered why he never got it.

Reasoner's noticed that all human endeavour is motivated by the desire for unconditional love, the most centered *feeling* with no thought movement. He who achieves or receives it *feels* he's the sexiest, coolest person. *Who wouldn't want that?* That's why industries are so interested in bottling and selling sexiness by brainwashing people with attainable images of stars. Anyone living with such a *feeling* could dwell in his body in the first person without longing for more or doubting his shortcomings. *Reasoner* believes that obtaining this *feeling* is what everyone wants: *If a person never gets to experience this, what's the point of life?* But even with the best PR team, it's hard to arrange being the sexiest person on the planet unless the closest hope is through virtual reality such as imagination and games.

If there could be one ultimate game, it'd be playing god. As god, the player would be able to make his own wishes come true, meaning the game would have to be perfectly flexible with plenty of programs to accommodate the player's desires. The drawback would be that the conventional God hasn't been able to shake off his unappealing image of being an old guy with a beard controlling the world, and so the game would likely become as limiting as current video games. Nevertheless, on the slight chance that such a god game could be developed, it'd be important to have a few preliminary guidelines:

1. Allows the player to have a first person experience with a full emotional spectrum.
2. Is dangerous and full of surprises, making the player feel he's participating in a real war, for instance.
3. Comes wirelessly interfaced with the player's body and six senses.
4. Comes with custom programming, so that he's able to accommodate anything he imagines.
5. Allows him to have sex with any partner he scores and it has to seem as real as real sex.
6. Has a surprise ending he can never guess.
7. Has an inherent hidden goal that he has to figure out.
8. Poses a mission so challenging that it might require many tries.
9. Is so realistic that he doesn't even know he's in a game, yet at the same time comes with a little loophole that allows him to realize he's in a game.

If a person could buy such a perfect game that met all of the above criteria, he'd finally be able to come true to his own wishes. He could be Elvis Presley or Bruce Lee instead of merely playing them as a game controller, just like he wouldn't choose video game sex over real sex. Or he could be a baby born with the potential of becoming anything he wanted.

Now Sok envisions he's the game player. He imagines he's lived his entire life never having realized the point of his miserable existence, though in reality he's been in a game. He envisages it's designed to disclose to him that one day he'll understand his life's only a game and that it makes it clear to him that that day is now. He imagines a game in which he isn't certain whether or not he's in the game, so that killing, fighting, eating, falling in love, falling ill, having a baby, losing loved ones or letting go of his life would necessarily feel real to him, just like crashing his car in a video game wouldn't devastate him since he knows it's virtual. So as not to spoil the suspense, Sok projects that he'll deliberate the playing of his game to allow himself to come to a dualistic view of experiencing life as reality while at the same time seeing it as a game. He visualizes that in order to have a fair chance of succeeding, he's blocked off certain out-of-game-characters from entering into the game such as angels with wings and gods with white hair who might trigger his insecurity, lead him to beg for mercy or make him forget he's in the game. To guarantee not becoming stuck in the game forever, he imagines programming it so that he'll die at some point. He projects that in order to make it feel real, he's set it up so that the only exit is death without the possibility of ever fully grasping that death itself might be an illusion. For his utmost excitement, he designs it so that he'll never know when or how the game will end, which will make it easier to enjoy every moment of the game. Completely accepting that the game might end at any second, he programs it to have enough challenging shit to *allow* him to surrender and enjoy the game in whatever state he's in. He imagines that in the game he grasps that if he doesn't get to understand his life might be just a game, he'll have spent it neither realizing he was in a game nor fathoming the point of his miserable existence.

Throughout his life, Sok's swung between his perceptions of viewing life as demanding of heavy toil, like shovelling the same old snow, or experiencing it as an alluring game replete with the joyful play of shovelling an amazing substance called snow. To enter into his perfect game whenever he wants all he needs to do is switch his perception. When he does he marvels at how much of a production it was to build the game set with snow spread out all over in front of him in such a large scale and with such quality of realism. The game's as real as it gets, since there's nothing that seems more real than reality. Sok knows that if he chooses to perceive his life with this detached perspective, there'll be no compromises in living out his wish to have the perfect game.

Reasoner's noticed that once Sok tasted the perception of life as a game, it simply became a matter of his choice whether to experience it as hell or paradise. Throughout history *Reasoner* hasn't found a single piece of evidence to prove that life's not a game deliberately designed to be a joy ride rather than a fateful accident. In addition, *Reasoner*'s aware of the existence of the *framework* with its implication that it might be one complete round of a game. Without being able to witness his own comings and goings, a person shouldn't be able to convince himself he's not in the game. If this were the case, the game player's tendency towards doubtful thinking would inevitably be defeated based on lack of evidence that his life wasn't planned, in which case his doubt would resign into *feeling* and invite *Triple Contrast*.

Within the game perception, when Sok no longer needs to convince himself of the difference between his present reality and his desire to find paradise in the perfect game, there ceases to be any more room for fantasizing, and he comes true to his desire to live within his present reality. If a person were unaware of the possibility that his life were merely a game, he might find the reality so harsh that he'd try to develop the perfect game so he could play it safely, one as realistic as the life-game he's already in. Even if he'd already developed his perfect game, he could still find it dissatisfying and eventually forget he was even in it. In that case, it's possible he'd feel the need to develop the next perfect game while he was already in this one. Very likely he'd feel the burden of also wanting it to be as realistic as the one he was already in, like the fate of Atlas who repeatedly carried the same burden on his shoulders without ever changing his reality.

Whenever Sok chooses to perceive his life as a game, he's awestruck at how it's being played out in front of him, and the seriousness of his reality fades away. Centered in his body and in an awakened state, he *sees* the world with renewed curiosity. *Reasoner* reflects that if Sok's life had been objectively difficult, *how would he have found it possible to enjoy himself as a kid, as in his childhood this reality was like waking himself up to* **Point B** *as his deepest wish came true?* *Reasoner*'s found that at the moment of switching perceptions, what Sok *sees* in front of him gets sharper as his *feeling* intensifies, giving him an impression similar to *deja vu*. Now that he resides within the game, he simply pursues what he wants happily, choosing to play the *Rider* and dooming everyone in the game with his pronouncement, *You've had all the chances in the world, but now it's too late!* He loves it.

Sok's painting, *Vertigo*, creates a similar visual impression. Sok focuses on it until he *feels* vertigo from the height. He's found it's easier to get the sensation if he imagines watching someone in one of the top floor balconies dropping a ball, and then he follows the ball all the way down with his eyes. The hypnotic effect shifts him into a different reality. The painting is a depiction of the numerous cookie-cutter apartment building complexes in Seoul, the patterns of which he remembers as mesmerizing. Next is the painting:

Eleventh Canvas: **Life as Theatre**

As the passage in Shakespeare's *As You Like It* goes:

All the world's a stage,
And all the men and women merely players;
They have their exits and their entrances,
And one man in his time plays many parts,
His acts being seven ages.

In light of a global perspective of human interactions, Sok finds Shakespeare's Globe Theatre relevant to his own creation of a *Quantum Theatre*. He'd even go so far as to say that within this limitless production, the whole universe is a stage, and everything animate or inanimate, actor or audience, are the players participating in one plot that can take millions of years or a second to complete in accordance with that individual's own directional and productional needs and preferences. In his lifetime a person enters and exits the plot, frequently becoming stuck somewhere along the way. The plot has its ebbs and flows, rises and falls, during which people find themselves protecting and destroying, cheating and confessing, selling out and walking out, falling into dependency and finding freedom, being sentimental and detached, saying hello and good-bye, killing and saving, calculating and saying *Fuck it*, thinking and feeling, perceiving the *known* and the *unknown*, or being born and dying.

Sok reflects that the plot is the *framework* that includes history, a person's life, a phase in his life, his relationships, his addictions, his ideals, his fashion, his projects, his travel, his moon cycle, his day, his sex, his drinking, his hangover, his eating, his nap, his arguments, his thoughts, his breathing. Each single plot fits into a larger plot, which in turn fits into a larger plot, like grains of sand on a beach that is itself a grain in a plot woven with billions of small plots, all plottings with different timings mixing to completion and concluding the larger plot. Small or large, each plot has the same *unknown-trust cycle* that can be condensed or stretched out into various shapes, like dough, as if reflected in the mirror maze of an amusement park. Each person's free to mix his own cocktail of plots within plots.

As Sok's mentioned earlier, from the onset every human being as one unit of a plot comes into the world with a feeling of raw vulnerability, due to his encounter with the *unknown* during the birth process. Normally he resists it. However, in the rare occasions that an entity like Terminator or god impersonator such as an ancient Egyptian pharaoh, is born with an acceptance of this most fundamental insecurity of the *unknown* experienced at birth, the equivalent of accepting death, then it's an act of love, most profoundly and powerfully spirited with the explosive *feeling* of beauty and sadness that's immensely moving and fulfilling and ends in complete trust. By facing up to the *unknown* at birth instead of submitting to fear, the *unknown-trust cycle* as the whole *framework* is completed, and that person's free to enter into a state of *oneness* even as a baby, like a god being impersonated on earth with a complete understanding of why he was born. Sok calls such a person the *Big Feelings Impersonator*. As that person completes the round from facing the *unknown* to having immediate and lasting trust, he experiences *Triple Contrast* at birth in all its explosive expansion. The completion of the *framework* begins at the moment of a person's acceptance of the *unknown* experienced as part of the birthing process. That acceptance is the reason to love for no reason. Unfortunately, however, from the very birth of their plots, people have a tendency to veer away from accepting the existential crisis of birth. The result is that they often end up living under a shroud of deep-rooted insecurity that transmogrifies into a fear of death.

Out of reaction to that familiar sinking feeling of fear that crops up repeatedly throughout people's lives and manifests at the global and individual level in increasingly pervasive bowel, stomach, kidney, liver, pancreas, heart and lung problems, people desperately latch onto something or someone, thus moving into chronically deepening phases of dependency, like a reaction of unstable chemicals. Most people spend their entire lives clinging to a false sense of security, coveting their feelings of uncertainty by building their realities based on fear and need. As if grabbing onto feeble grass floating on the raft of life in a frantic attempt to delay the inevitable inching towards death, they never have to deal directly with the most fundamental fear of being alone in the universe. As time goes by, this collective human dependency subsides into what's perceived as a manageable rise and fall in smaller plots, like a person picking up a pebble he likes and holding onto it until he finally decides to fling it. But at the dawn of the apocalypse, unless people are willing both individually and collectively to "lift the veil" from their tightly constructed realities, they won't confront their fear of the *unknown* until either individual death or the cosmic catastrophe hits. This evasion of the *unknown* thrusts people and the planet into a *death cycle*, like the fading of a flower at the end of summer or the turning of autumn leaves in the return cycle of the seasons.

Deeply embedded in a person's need to cling to dependency is the lost knowledge of self-trust that he came out okay through the birth process. Invariably he forgets that although his birth was collective work between his mother and himself, ultimately, it was he who chose to be born and that birthing into the next *framework* always hinges on a person's individual choice. He fails to acknowledge his own autonomy as an independent being in the universe who birthed himself through the sheer will of his own life force. Instead he succumbs to a desperate desire for dependency and initiates a *death cycle*, becoming entirely death-oriented through his avoidance of the *unknown* until the time of his actual death, which he perceives and therefore manifests through his fear as annihilation. However, arresting the *death cycle* through an intensity of experience that approximates death equals coming into proximity with birth so that the existential dilemma can be naturally negated at both ends. If a person's able to accept the *unknown* of death while he's still alive, he'll be overwhelmed by a profound sensation of beauty and sadness. The fading of this *feeling* concludes one cycle of the old *framework*, and a new *unknown-trust cycle* begins.

Sok reflects that the cycle of personal plots can be applied to human history. The beginning of the historical cycle is always instigated by a trauma such as Cain reacting to his own trauma by killing Abel. Between the beginning and end of the cycle, dramas are acted out that constitute the interacting network of everyone's collective traumas. Sok sees that the aim of the plot is first to be enriched with as many trauma-generating dramas as possible and then to finish in one cycle. For the final act, the players have to accept all of their individual and collective traumas in order not to have any more dramas to play out. Within the overall plot of history there are many small plots with which to be dealt. Ultimately the macrocosm of history and the microcosm of an individual's life constitute the shape of history, just as a person's cells collectively make up the larger self, or the state of the world's oceans reflects the internal liquid environment of a human, animal, plant or micro-organism's body. Sok understands that the loop of history is the larger triangle of *Triple Contrast* that includes every individual entity's life.

Within the larger triangle, history is *Triple Contrast: Feelings, Thoughts* and *Awareness*. Sok calls the lump sum of humanity's feelings *Big Feelings* and the lump sum of humanity's thoughts *Big Thoughts*; with the inclusion of *Awareness*, these three elements combined constitute one cycle of human history. The *framework* begins with *Big Feelings*, continues through the *Big Thoughts* of every human drama and ends in *Triple Contrast*. *Triple Contrast* is the well-developed collective human brain capacity of *Big Thoughts* accepting *Big Feelings* within the *Triangle of Awareness*. Simply speaking, *Big Triple Contrast* is when people all over the world choose on their own to accept their life traumas and live in the present without feeling the need to instigate any more dramas.

Big Feelings are the rough draft of history within the *framework*, like a daydream of what's to come. They're the collective *feelings* of humanity generated by the convergence of every individual's traumas throughout history with a million subtle variations of responses originating from a fundamental sense of foreboding or *feeling* of death. They're the counterpart of *Big Thoughts*, the collective memory tank of everyone's lifelong dramas combined throughout history, like the film archives of everyone's acts throughout their lives and history, or like the hard drive of a computer.

Sok ventures to speculate that at the dawn of human history when archetypical humans were confronted with *Big Feelings* (death, the collective *feeling* of the *unknown*), they would unlikely have been able to grasp *Big Thoughts* and *Big Feelings* simultaneously, like the Big Bang or the booting up of a Mac computer. But Sok imagines they could've had instant enlightenment at birth and inherently known birth and death as the same transitional state. Nevertheless, unlike people today who have the potential to comprehend the entire gamut of history, primitive man was as yet incapable of grasping the entire picture in order to understand the loop of history and *Big Triple Contrast* instantaneously. In this sense, early humans being unable to grasp the Big Picture must've been like the very first computer trying to play a movie with state-of-the-art resolution. Sok conjectures that primitive man's so-called limited capacity wasn't due to his evolutionary design. It's just that evolution takes time because it entails one entity die with a trauma-based need or wish that gets reflected in his next return, which isn't the same as a baby in one lifetime evolving to grow a tail. For a wish to come to completion, a being or entity has first to endure the frustration of living through the opposite of what he wants in reality. That's survival of the fittest, as when a smaller fish that's eaten by a bigger fish causes a trauma that triggers a desire to have a sting or be faster, like the drive to create new state-of-the-art software.

At the beginning of history, the *framework* was like the rough draft of a script handed out to actors in the form of fetus-to-human-to-something else. It was an outline of human dramas, stories, legends, myths and fairytales found within the histories of every culture. Just as the first traumatized *T* played his role as a victimized individual unaware that his *Small Thoughts* were mere fragments broken off from the *Big Triangle*, he would've been unable to fathom *Big Feelings*. He wouldn't have been capable of trusting that his own insecurity, fear and mistrust were the reasons history would still take eons to play itself out. Sok ponders that like all feelings, *Big Feelings* are timeless in that unlike *Big Thoughts*, they're complete from the beginning. At the onset of the plot, *Big Feelings* would've been like mythical gods in comparison to *T*. The reason Sok understands the existence of *Big Feelings* as being the teachers of humanity stems from the fact that human beings throughout history have emphasized the importance of learning, which implies there's something to be taught. But the one lesson people haven't yet learned is to accept death, which requires they learn to conceive of death as birth within one *framework* that reflects the most fundamental *unknown-trust cycle* of coming into life from the *unknown* during conception to developing in the womb as a fetus and finally being born as a baby. The most qualified teacher of this *birth-death-birth cycle* would be a wild animal mother kicking her grown babies out of the nest to fend for themselves in order to cut short or eliminate the middle stage of dependency so that the *unknown-trust cycle* of birth and death can meet. Such a wise teacher might actually be able to push the human race onto the Titanic so that it can face its doom and rise to the impending apocalyptic challenge.

The spectrum of human emotions has been reflected in Greek tragedies, as well as carved in traditional Japanese noh masks and played out on the noh stage as dramatic presentations of *T*'s trauma-based lessons. Life after life, generation after generation, *T*'s grown in his capacity to the point of being able to face *Big Feelings* (death) and conclude the historical *Big Plot*. Finally *T*'s become the *Rider*. At the end of the *framework* Sok's *Rider* has reemerged through history and now resides in the *Big Triangle*, replete with the scripted software of every role he's ever enacted at his disposal to play with as he pleases.

Next are thirteen mug shots of Sok's twelve characters, the last one being Sok himself. From his life sagas of playing his characters inside and out, he's chiseled out twelve characteristic expressions of himself, like Japanese noh masks. He believes that documenting or carving his spectrum of facial expressions equals being finally able to see himself with an air of detachment. He'll never again allow himself to be ruled by his emotions. Like an actor who's learned to act from tapping into his past emotions and learning how to control them, Sok's become master of his own beast.

Hedonist　　　　　　　　　　　*Martyr*

Hermit　　　　　　　　　　　*Reasoner*

Clown　　　　　　　　　　　*Warrior*

Believer

Killer

Victim/Saviour

Destroyer/Sabotager

Junkie/Addict

Skeptic

Sok

Twelfth Canvas: **Roles in the Plot**

1 Flying a B-29 Bomber Over Korea at Night & Looking Up at a Piece of Sky

According to the dualistic way human beings perceive themselves, everyone can be cast into two basic roles, like black and white, dark and light, yin and yang, devils and angels. Although this might seem to be a human theatre lacking in complex character roles, none is quite the same because everyone concocts his or her own unique blend of being either a *Blamer* or a *Claimer*.

Blamers like Sok's dad blame everyone and everything except themselves for receiving their traumas, whereas *Claimers* like Sok claim their own responsibility for creating theirs. However, most people fall within the vast spectrum of grey, leaning towards a dominant role with varying degrees of purity. Within the smaller plots people are constantly moving in and out of one or the other extreme: a *Claimer*, when interacting with a purer *Claimer*, can take on the role of *Blamer*, like a person who would assume a doormat persona at work while going back home to yell at his kids who are pure *Claimers*; on the other hand, a *Blamer* can take on the role of *Claimer*, pretending to go along with the intention of getting his dad's inheritance.

In their purest forms at polar ends of the *Blamer/Claimer* spectrum are *Killers* and *Martyrs*. Within the larger plot of history, they're the ones who instigate the passing of traumas between the two extremes, just as the pull of the North and South Poles churn the currents of the seas. In the human theatre, the plot is the movement of passing on traumas. It runs in a circular motion from birth to death, just as an abused child grows up to harass his own child, who'll in turn retaliate by getting back at his own children or dad in his old age. The plot has a *quantum* script that functions as a rough directional guide to a person's life, like the force of a flowing river draining into the ocean to disappear as one cycle of history in the horizontal loop of the *framework*. Passing down traumas from one generation to the next is like the current of a river, the norm being that most people will continue to react throughout their lives to keep the flow. But on rare occasions, if one person chooses to accept his trauma, he'll break the cycle and at once complete the lesson of human history, like Jesus or Buddha.

Sok's found that whether people become *Blamers* or *Claimers* hinges on where they're positioned within the three stages of the plot: birth, dependency and death. Their roles are determined by how strongly they resist each stage of movement towards the completion of the plot. Particularly *Blamers* have accepted their birth traumas, just as 007 overcame being an orphan. They tend not to have received much parental nurturing, often undergoing hardship or growing up in unloving hostile environments. As a result, they become self-sufficient and quite capable of acting independently. As they go through traumatic incidents that remind them of their birth traumas of the *unknown*, they learn all by themselves to accept the pileup of disasters that have begun early on in their lives. Since they never got to experience the sweet paradise of being nurtured by their mothers, they grow up reacting to everything with a single-minded worldview. According to a *Blamer*, everyone's an asshole, and the only person he can depend on is himself.

Due to the fact that from the onset, *Blamers* accept their traumatic state as the norm, they belong to the beginning stage of the plot movement when the uncertainty of birth hasn't yet turned into full dependency. Poised between feelings of insecurity (which they've partially accepted) and their lack of dependency, they're seemingly awake, confident and charismatic. However, Sok's found that within their built-in blaming characteristic, *Blamers* have a blind spot in that they don't see how they're the creators of their own traumas, which hinders them from becoming choice makers.

As is the case of everyone, *Blamers'* traumas, including their birth traumas, are the result of their choice not to trust, despite the fact that *Blamers* have more potential to embrace the *unknown* based on the intensity of their early traumas. But since they still aren't fully able to believe in themselves, they end up constantly striving, like guiltless godlike slaves, passing on all of their traumas to *Claimers* and pushing everyone towards the *death cycle*. From their opportunistic point of view, everyone else is doing the same thing as them, so with the conviction that success is at the expense of everyone, and everything is fair game, they can be relaxed, objective learners and efficacious life players. A *Blamer* is a role model of how to be a true asshole; in his most benign persona, he's like the two-faced news anchor type depicted in movies.

Sok's observed through himself and others that unlike *Blamers*, *Claimers* (including *Martyrs*, the ultimate *Claimers*) have experienced the paradise of good nurturing, and consequently, live with a feeling of trust that birth isn't annihilation until a subsequent trauma hits, at which point their reaction is usually a confused mixture of self-trust and the second stage of dependency. In general, *Claimers* claim responsibility for their traumas, mainly because they fail to see that drawing on the wall or pissing their pants has caused them all of a sudden to fall victim to *Blamer* punishment. Often feeling they're the causes of their troubles, they develop a keen moral sense of right and wrong. Being unable to find justification for their sudden descent into hell, they react by blaming themselves. Having experienced both paradisal and hellish extremes, as well as the full spectrum of emotions in between, they spend the rest of their lives swinging from self-doubt based on the contrast between paradise and hell to a suppressed desire to return the abuse to the harasser, which gets played out mostly in their fantasies. When this happens *Claimers* start learning how to blame and play out their reverse roles by taking their emotions out on those weaker than them.

Claimers comprise the vast majority of the population and are totally reliant on how *Blamers* such as parents, teachers, controlling spouses, CEO's and nation presidents perceive them. Out of reaction to their own feelings of vulnerability, *Claimers* refuse to let go of their mother's breasts, security blankets or anything else they've been cling-ing to, opting instead to play the role of naive children, while at the same time concealing their feelings of anger at themselves for being too gutless to make a change or harass their harassers. As they've also never accepted the trauma and insecurity of birth, they go through life swaying confusedly between the concepts of trust and luck. In a state of constant denial, they act as if they're procrastinating on their weekend homework, often playing sleepy characters while daydreaming about becoming successful *Blamers*. *Claimers* are everywhere, buying lottery tickets and gambling in casinos armed with luck, while *Blamers* are the ones running the joints and tampering with the odds so they always win, or at least playing the stock market, their preferred forum of gam-bling because it's more controlled. *Claimers* tend to be blind to all this *Blamer* activity, however, blaming their losses on bad luck, fate or family.

Sok's noticed that among *Blamers*, *Killers* have usually experienced some kind of severe trauma such as being victims of attempted murder, on top of their initial harsh beginning as neglected *Blamers*. Within the experiential spectrum of paradise and hell, this positions them on the hell extreme since they haven't encountered paradise. However, due to the contrast between their two hellish traumatic experiences (their harsh *Blamer* beginning and having been the victim of attempted murder), *Killers* are riddled with self-doubt. Sok's observed the greater the contrast *Killers* experience between their hellish extremes, the more doubtful they become as to how severe their reactions should be. They're torn between executing the milder harassment of regular *Blamers* or staging a massacre for their core satisfaction as *Killers*. This is true of a lot of North Koreans, Vietnamese and Cambodians who've been taken away from their parents as children and thrown into continuous life threatening circumstances. In certain cases, those deep-rooted doubts turn into superficial questions not concerning whether they'll kill, but how many people they should mass murder. Such considerations are motivated by self-doubt and hinge on the contrast between the severities of their traumas. Sometimes having two conflicting life goals can even become their drive to find a more balanced aim so that they can more comfortably settle into their lives, like a *Killer* using his murderous urge to become an aggressive businessman as his life goal instead of actually killing, or some other way that he can happily carry on his abusive lifestyle. Whether or not *Killers* accept this impulse determines two types: *Criminals* and followers of the *Big Feelings Impersonator*.

Sok's observed that *Criminals* swing between being *Killers* and martyr-like *Blamers*. Sok sees that sometimes they can act as a *Martyr* or vigilante like Dexter, whom everyone views as a nice guy. As *Criminals* generally slack off on their task of needing to clarify their life purpose, they continue to live on as confused individuals. They're often unlucky and unsuccessful because of their doubtful nature and typically end up becoming murderers, serial *killers*, or in Dexter's case, a vigilante serial-*killer*. Sok knows that when *Criminals* are in their more reactive cycle, like werewolves under a full moon, they act out being the foot soldiers of *Big Feelings* by going on killing sprees designed to fuel fear. Or they might take a different route of following their dark impulses towards gaining clarity by becoming followers of *Big Feelings* such as religious leaders, world leaders, dictators, politicians, toxin manufacturers or businessmen. Such supporters of the *Big Feelings Impersonator* resist short-term satisfaction in order to shed doubts and gain purity by holding back their murderous impulses over the long term. As in the cases of Napoleon Bonaparte and Adolf Hitler, their work can lead them to be viewed as heroes by some and mass murderers by others.

Sok's criminal-oriented aspect of himself is often attracted to the exhilaration of committing a heinous crime. He imagines the sensation being like a male virgin fantasizing on his first experience of penetration. One of the things that separates Sok from *Criminals*, however, is that he uses the medium of his painting to create certain horrifying visual sensations of actions such as dropping a bomb over a densely populated area. Sok's next painting satisfies this realm of his imagination by depicting the experience of flying a bomber over two densely populated hills in Korea after midnight. The two hilltops closest to the eyes of the pilot are made up of larger sized roofs, in comparison to the smaller sized houses at the bottoms of the hills. The title of the painting is *Flying a B29 Bomber Over Korea at Night*.

Unlike *Blamers, Killers* and *Criminals,* Sok's perceived that *Martyrs* (the ultimate *Claimers*) accept personal responsibility for their own hellish circumstances and gravitate towards the death cycle by internalizing their traumas as their only option. Within the plot they stand on the receiving end of their traumas so that they don't have anyone except themselves to blame or pass them onto. As they're disinclined to externalize them by taking revenge, as *Blamers* do, they're compelled towards death, which they unconsciously perceive as their only way of returning to paradise. However, Sok's found that as they're hesitant to cross that bridge of death, they redirect their death wishes to acts of masochism or self-sabotage. Samuel Beckett in *Rough Theater 1* sums up the *martyr* dilemma as follows:

B: *Why don't you kill yourself? Why don't you kill yourself?*
A: *I've thought of it... I'm not unhappy enough.*

In most cases, as *Martyrs* are unable to go through with suicide as their ultimate revenge, *You'll be sorry when I'm gone!* they end up gradually destroying themselves and their health through self-abuse and depression from their accumulation of traumas and eventually die from the weight of them. Sok casts them into the external *Martyr* roles of masochists, junkies, whores or internal *Martyrs* such as hypochondriacs. Based on the human dynamic, Sok's observed that throughout history, *Martyrs* (one aspect of who Jesus was, for instance) have irked the killing urge in people, especially those *Claimers* looking for a chance to play the role of *Blamers*, like chickens pecking on the weak or the mob of Jesus followers and Peter, who at the last minute turned against Jesus in an act of self-betrayal. On the other hand, *Martyrs* are attracted to *Blamers* because of their craving for abuse. Sok's found the perfect example in two types of Catholic priests: the child molester type who's a *Claimer* pecking on weaker *Claimers*, and the *Blamer* political money-oriented variety who abuses everyone with his guilt-tripping sermons.

Blamers recognize that *Claimers* possess a unique quality that's fundamentally different from what *Blamers* have possessed since birth. *Blamers* instinctively understand the weaknesses of *Claimers*, and given their strong appetite for life, perceive no conflict between what they want to do in their private thoughts and what they're willing to do in reality. The main drive of *Blamers* is to intimidate and bully *Claimers* so as to make them even more insecure and dependent. *Blamers* do it joyfully, however they can, with fists, laws, logic, morals, philosophy, religion and education.

Sok's noticed that with their appetite for life, *Blamers* of the *Criminal* variety go about the fear-based business of killing in service of *Blamers* and *Big Feelings*, the bullying teachers of humanity. For example, a few deaths can churn up and reset the circulation of the economy to increase people's dependency on insurance, media, government, security systems and improved weapons. Inevitably for *Blamers* such as business owners and manufacturers, the end result is a financial reshuffling of their hand in the poker game. Sok's witnessed *Blamers* using fear as a pilot for generating hope to lure *Claimers* in by instilling them with optimism.

With their trustworthy trademark of managing future justice as respected members of society, *Blamers* sugarcoat hopelessness as hope for a general public mostly comprised of weaselly *Claimers*. To harass them, *Blamers* indulge in the secret pleasure of enforcing laws based on moral justice onto the majority of *Claimers* who guiltily comply with the prospect of gaining improved conditions in the future. The success of their strategy is based on *Claimers'* tendency to depend on and be intimidated by *Blamers*, which blinds them from questioning whether *Blamer's future* promises will ever materialize. Meanwhile, *Blamers* are pretty much guaranteed their minimal effort will result in success. By blinding *Claimers* with hope, *Blamers* enjoy unlimited freedom to conduct experiments on the planet and the public, as in the case of medical doctors, who are dependent on the pharmaceutical industry to peddle ineffective, toxic cancer "cures" such as chemotherapy, radiation treatments and whatever else, despite surveys of leading oncologists within the medical profession and at leading universities who confess that if they were diagnosed with cancer, they'd reject conventional cancer treatments, based on statistical studies and their empirical observations that chemotherapy is inhumane, ineffective and detrimental. Nevertheless, *Blamers* intuitively understand there's no such thing as failure because their aim is that with minimal effort they can generate future optimism. Within the *framework* of history, Sok understands that traumas generated by *Big Feelings* are mere perpetuations of future hope based on a current consensus of hopelessness.

Sok understands that *Blamers* are the foot soldiers of the *Big Feelings Impersonator (BFI)*, who throughout history has been the CEO of the planet. Together they've established that a chain of command is the most effective tool to generate hope. Once *BFI* creates a pecking order with himself on top, everyone else falls into the pyramid of entertaining prospects of being the first someday. Throughout history, religion's been the most successful tool for placing *Claimers* at the bottom of the ladder in opposition to their self-imposed god, the *Big Feelings Impersonator*, with whom no one can obtain equal footing. Within the scheme of things, despite its wholesome front, education is the darkest competitive social reality. This is most apparent in Asia, where the drive for educational superiority has replaced the traditional feudal system. Asian *Blamers* understand this, and so to support the validity of competitive education, they hire only a few highly qualified *Claimers* to justify paying pittance to the rest of the majority of *Claimers* who are made to feel they're somehow lacking in credentials or whatever else. In addition, new religions such as science, medicine and pharmaceuticals all sell so-called cures while funding scientists, doctors and the business of finding cures that may or may not work someday, as if they're opening the most expensive champagne with the hope of success rather than actual achievement. Meanwhile, lawyers and politicians pursue law and order within justice systems that with any luck will bring fairness someday.

Sok's noticed that *Blamers* don't even need to work at maintaining their scams because everyone reacts to traumas. With hopes of understanding the fucked-up-ness of the world, *Claimers* voluntarily polish and maintain their morals, principles and philosophies, all reflections of their traumas. They react to *Blamers'* scams with moral judgment by enforcing constipating principles and philosophical confusion, while *Blamers* by nature don't give a shit about morals, principles and philosophy. *Claimers* love this bullshit and are addicted to images of the Ideal Blamer of the Week, some movie star, or politician, onto whom they can glom and hope to mimic within a few weeks. Particularly Asian *Claimers* shop themselves to death, buying name brands to give the impression of being well-to-do *Blamers*. Nevertheless, Sok knows that the treatment for this incurable disease is doom because it eradicates the breeding ground for hope. There are even some *Martyrs* such as him who take on this task of dooming.

From personal experience, Sok knows that certain *Martyrs* have experienced the same severity of trauma as *Killers*. Among all the characters in the *Quantum Theatre*, these *Martyrs* understand the momentous contrast between paradise and hell, which makes them the most driven of any of the other characters in the *Quantum Theatre*. Like sperm, they have the strongest motivation to get what they want. *Extreme Martyrs* like Sok either don't last long due to their destructiveness, or alternatively find a way to accept death. They play the most doubtful unluckiest characters. When *Martyrs* don't accept death, they remain as nerds, but when they do accept the prospect of their own annihilation, they embark on a bipolar journey of vacillating between being *Killers* or *Martyrs*. In the best case scenario, they settle into a more detached state of offering themselves up to be harassed simply as an experiment, resembling the behaviour of some autistic children. In their fierce devotion to shed their doubts caused by their knowledge of the contradiction between paradise and hell, and with an arsenal of bad luck in magical proportions, they stifle their urge to kill, be killed or kill themselves until they decide to move on to the next experiment of shedding their doubts one at a time. They tend to be non-judgmental, since they can't afford to become *Killers* through the act of condemning their harassers. The depth of their depression and desperation causes them to feel that obtaining permanent answers is more important than finding temporary emotional satisfaction.

Sok knows there are other *Extreme Martyrs* with the potential to break free from the *Big Feelings Impersonator*—some writers, visual artists, performers, musicians, actors, philosophers—the few apolitical, original and often terribly unsuccessful ones, whose work is neither a reflection of nor reaction to society, but rather is self-oriented. In Sok's opinion, any reflective or reactive work is a form of aggression, the result of people playing their reverse role to become their former abusers. Therefore, it's as unoriginal as what their abusers did to them. He thinks this process is valid; nevertheless, he believes that the definition of art is overcoming that state. However, when people surmount that reactive state of role reversal, they become experts at internalizing their traumas, as are all *Martyrs*, yet balanced with an external *Killer* side. Having accepted their path towards death, they've awakened to the idea that they might as well express what they want, regardless of what anybody else thinks, by playing out their *Killer* side as callously as they can with the *Awareness* of being killed, rather than actually killing themselves while lying depressed in their beds. Sok reflects that an *Extreme Martyr* is the kid in the fairytale, *The Emperor's Clothes*, because regular adult *Claimers* and *Blamers* wouldn't normally blow the whistle that the Emperor was naked out of fear that the Emperor might retaliate against them and their families. On the other hand, *Extreme Martyrs* are always willing to disturb the shit without a thought about their own death; in fact, not only do they secretly tend towards self-destruction, but also they don't care much about any-one else's demise, including that of their own family members who were playing the role of *Blamers* while *Extreme Martyrs* were growing up as *Martyrs*, like Cinderella's stepmother and stepsisters.

When *EMs* gain back their trustful childlike innocence, they're detached and straightforward since it's a given they've never been liked in the first place. So with nothing to lose, they're free. This is when they achieve the state of *Trinity*, in which a person can conjure up *Triple Contrast* at will to grasp the whole *framework* in complete acceptance of death, and therefore, in trust. This is the point when *Extreme Martyr* is poised between internalizing himself as *Martyr* and externalizing himself as *Killer*. He becomes the *Rider*, who Sok views as the counterpart of the *Big Feelings Impersonator*. While *BFI* creates as many traumas as he can to enrich the plot, the *Rider* knows how to overcome those traumas to complete the *Big Plot* successfully. The *Big Plot* of history's like a person taking a trip with a poisonous snakebite while holding the antidote in his hand.

Sok understands that coming up with a solution to the human predicament is collective work. Prompted by traumas brought on by the *Big Feelings Impersonator*, *Blamers* and *Claimers* have to maintain their dramas to drive away and confine *Extreme Martyr* in his dungeon where he becomes so utterly bored and bothered that he might as well take on the challenging and satisfying task of dooming everyone else.

During the continuing sagas involving endless rallies of revenge, *Claimers* believe in justice and the concept of good while condemning others. *Blamers*, on the other hand, don't believe in justice; like criminal lawyers, they're able to see both the kettle and the pot between *Claimers* (who are reacting passive-aggressively to create a lot of victims with minor traumas) and *Killers* and *Criminals* (who are actively creating fewer victims with stronger traumas). In the name of justice and for their own gain, *Blamers* lock up *Criminals* to maintain *Claimers'* faith in the system. *Claimers* are the majority of people who don't run the world and don't have any particular personal angle on it either.

When *Claimers* and *Martyrs* don't take responsibility for finding out why traumas happen in their lives, they remain hypocritical by reacting constantly, blaming others for their miseries. For driving away *Extreme Martyrs*, nothing's as effective as *Claimer* hypocrisy. Hypocrisy boils the blood of *Killers* and *Extreme Martyrs* since it confuses them in their path of shedding doubts. Ultimately *Extreme Martyrs* remain the only exception because they're simply incapable of bearing their hypocritical selves when they become conscious that they're reacting.

As adults, both *Killers* and *Extreme Martyrs* are believers of dark fairy-tales. They see themselves standing alone against a world full of assholes, who once instilled in everyone a belief in fairytales, but now sneer at those who still believe. *Killers* fantasize themselves to be antagonistic fairytale characters no different from real life villains. As they gain greater purity of purpose, they might come to see the world as a fantasy-like reality game and a more desirable alternative to daydreaming. Freshly awakened, they leave their fantasies behind and begin to live in the present as real villains. Furthermore, *Killers* never take responsibility for their choices, crediting luck, god or spirits as their driving force. *BFI*, the boss of all *Killers*, is the only one who doesn't have a conflict of interest since he understands the overall plot within the *framework*. He's the dark fairy godmother who grants people's wishes by stranding them on the Titanic, which he knows is the equivalent of them all coming true to their wishes, and therefore, no longer having to wish.

Sok also refers to the *Big Feelings Impersonator* as *Trinity*. Due to his instantaneous grasping of the *framework* at birth, he's never experienced the insecurity of birth and its chain of dependency. He's always been completely awake and had full access to the *Big Plot* or *framework*, just as Jesus achieved later on after a life of self-searching. However, *BFI* never engages in self-questioning or soul-searching because he's an entity with no concept of apology. Like Terminator, on being born he already knows what to do within the *framework*. This powerful sorcerer becomes an enforcer of the *Big Plot*, one of the teachers of *Big Feelings*. Like a god, he creates traumas everywhere for his own personal gain, using the lessons of humanity as his playground. Sok's envisages *BFI* to be the CEO of the planet, a god-like cunning old man who's the enforcer behind the *framework* and prompts the collective traumas of history to fill in *Big Thoughts*. Sok understands *BFI* to have a certain omniscient control over the direction and intention of people's lives, just as a casino owner would set up his business for the purpose of making money under the guise of running his joint purely for entertainment.

Similarly, Sok sees the same pattern in the *Bible*. The *Bible* possesses incredible depth in its meanings and lessons passed on by enlightened people; however, there must've been a corruptive force behind its making that manipulated everything by incorporating the third-person God into the narrative. Sok imagines that negative force to be the work of *Big Feelings Impersonator*, the controlling entity behind religious leaders that twisted the *Bible*'s words of wisdom by incorporating himself as God and deviously embedded a hierarchical dependency into the biblical narrative. To use a more current example, the general way in which today's businesses are run reveals an overall destructive global intention. *Who could possibly be running the planet on such a momentous scale except* **BFI***, the enforcer of the framework, who oversees the collective traumas of history to complete the* **Quantum Theatre***? BFI* is like God in the *Bible* or Sauron, the Dark Lord of Mordor, in J.R.R. Tolkien's *Lord of the Rings*, that invisible timeless controlling teacher and evil force behind everything.

At the opposite end of the spectrum from *BFI, Extreme Martyr* is so deficient in his external relationships that he's unable to witness his own manifestation; on the other hand, in his role of externally manifesting traumas, *BFI* craves the reclusive internalized world of *EM*. Being *EM* himself, Sok knows that what recreates his own paradise is his internal makeup, consisting of two elements:

1. Sok's lifelong habit of daydreaming has allowed him to identify the most satisfying state within the details of his fantasies. His one and only wish has been to have his own external playground, just like *BFI*. Therefore, *EM*'s ultimate wish turns out to be an internalized reflection of *BFI*'s external playground, initially fostered through traumas instilled by *BFI*;

2. Sok's intelligence, cultivated through having access to the *unknown-trust cycle*, has enabled him to figure out how to manifest his internal playground externally, like a mad person spending his entire life trying to transform into a fairy godmother. However, *EM* knows that if he gives up pursuing his dream, he's destined to die from the weight of his own depression caused by internalizing traumas passed on by *BFI*. If that happens, *BFI* will gladly add *EM*'s life footage to his archives. According to *BFI*'s wishful scenerio, *EM*'s fate is either to die of depression or commit suicide. However, the fact that *EM* has already completed his own internal structure and is willing to die for his dream lends him the intelligence to know that in order to manifest his playground externally, he has to let go of his entire internal *EM* makeup. In this way *EM*'s able to use his drive to let go of his sweet fantasy world, at which point he transforms into the *Rider* and discloses his internal playground to the external world. As soon as he does, death and rebirth come to him simultaneously, and his old *framework* flashes before his eyes at the same time as he's rebirthing to a new one. It's like waking up to an altered reality. It's *Seeing Horses*.

EM wakes up to enjoy his playground and play externally, beginning by exposing everyone else to the truth that *BFI*'s a powerless naked emperor, since without having people's wishes to prey upon, he simply can no longer act on his own. In this way, *EM* fulfills his dream of externalizing his *Killer* side by blowing the whistle and creating a dooming effect on everyone else. Sok visualizes these opposing, yet cooperative forces of *BFI* and *EM* as creating a spiral movement, like the spinning of a revolving door. This is *Point B*.

Sok sees *Point B* as the marriage between *BFI*'s horizontal, fear-driven, future-oriented movement in time within the circular motion of the *framework* and *EM*'s converse vertical, love-based, trusting pull of timelessness, like a whirlpool over a drain. As *EM* internalizes his traumas that have been occurring along the horizontal timeline from his babyhood to adulthood, he stacks those memories to which he has timeless access, like accessing individual chapters on a dvd. Although he could've reacted to those traumas as they were happening, since he didn't yet understand their purpose, he held them in quarantine instead, all the while banking his time to build up his capacity. After voluntarily accepting his own death without any more traumas to internalize, he witnesses his past visions materializing in front of him and is finally awake to act out externally. The total sum of his memories is the completion of one historical cycle of Cain to Sok. This is *Big Triple Contrast*, through which Sok begins to *see* the external world through the prism of *Big Feelings*, like booting up a new Mac as his new *framework* of trust. At this point, *EM*'s perception becomes the same as that of *BFI*, who since birth has witnessed the world within the *framework* of *Big Triple Contrast*. Ultimately Sok understands that when *EM* externalizes this internal timelessness on a historical scale, he pulls the horizontal circling of time vertically, initiating a whirlpool effect, the 3-D expression of love and creation, like the shell of a snail.

Next is one of Sok's paintings that captures this spiral movement. Its title is *Looking Up at a Piece of Sky*. While Sok was painting he focused on deepening his *feelings* and witnessed their manifestation twisting his visual perspective, like a cat's tail.

According to Sok's perception, the spiral has its initial diverging point between *EM*'s vertical timeless movement and *BFI*'s horizontal force. As *BFI*'s horizontal power diminishes, *EM* wakes up fully to infiltrate his perception of horizontal temporality towards the end of the world with the vertical timelessness of a new beginning. For choice makers, the duration of the spiraling movement from beginning to end is equal to the time needed to enter into the highest frequency of timelessness. It's the duration from having a sense of *Point B* in the present to actualizing it in the future. *Point B* is at the centre of a spiral-like pointy end of a caracole, where over the span of history *EMs* have the capacity for being balanced within the cycle of birth and death. In this way, they have external timeless access to history in *Triple Contrast*, just as if it were a 3D-DVD. That's the outcome of all the collective work in the universe. That's *Triple Contrast*.

2 Sok's Take on Jesus

Sok's interested in applying his psychological insights to the spectrum between *Blamers* and *Claimers* in order to unravel the man who throughout history has evoked the most curiosity and controversy. In so doing, he reflects his own *EM* psychological profile onto the *martyr* Jesus as a building block out of which to devise Sok's own version of Jesus' life.

Sok sees that for Jesus to end up playing the messiah persona, he must've experienced a trauma that was diametrically opposed to his future reality. The opposite of becoming a messiah is being a victim in the early stages of becoming an *Extreme Martyr*. If ever there was a historical persona who displayed the most typical *EM* qualities it was Jesus, as he demonstrated later in his life when he was so attracted to death that he didn't even mind being killed in the worst imaginable way. As in Sok's case, and in light of the mythical story surrounding Jesus' nativity, his originating *EM* trauma very likely revolved around his mother, the *Virgin Mary*, within the paradigm of paradise and hell that Sok's previously mapped out.

Sok isn't convinced by Christianity's claim that Jesus' mom, Mary, was a virgin. He reflects that most likely before marrying Joseph, Mary had sex with someone else and then gave birth to the bastard Jesus. *Why else would she have given birth to Jesus in a manger?* Upon further consideration of the Catholic invention of the virgin mother, Sok asserts that if *BFI* wanted to inflict traumas to make everyone feel guilty and insecure, the best way to do it would be to fabricate dramas revolving around sex. By promoting asexual religious icons originating with Mary and Jesus, and reinforced by priests and nuns, everyone else is compelled to feel guilty by not ever being allowed to have sexual thoughts, let alone exhibit erroneous sexual behaviour such as masturbation. *God resides in your thoughts,* say the cold sexless priests and nuns. Sok believes the fact that Mary was a virgin was the first of many manipulations of the Catholic Church.

That Jesus' mom most likely had an affair and made a regretful decision to have sex before marriage suggests she could've been a *Claimer* who followed her heart, and that possibly Jesus was her love child. That and the fact that according to the *Bible*, Jesus' birth and infancy were not only sheltered, but also celebrated by shepherds and wise men bearing gifts, imply that at the beginning of his life he experienced paradise.

Historical records of Buddha indicate he underwent a similar pattern of initially experiencing paradise as a young prince who was overprotected by his dad, the king. The king reacted on the omen of a wise man who predicted that once his son saw four signs, he'd become a teacher instead of following in the footsteps of his father and taking the throne. One of the signs was death. At that point in his childhood, Buddha was so pampered that the extent of his suffering had been witnessing his fawn dying. Apparently he was the king of all the brats. Thanks to the king's efforts to shield Buddha from even witnessing death, Buddha had no concept that someday he'd also die. Likewise, as legend indicates, the love child, Jesus, must've enjoyed receiving special attention from his parents and other people, both humble and revered, who came from far and wide to bless his birth. As the Christmas songs and rituals attest, everything points to his experience of warmth, love and popularity at birth, *So what went wrong to make him* **EM***? At what point did Jesus descend into hell?*

Mary was wed by Joseph, who from the perspective of the times must've been a true *Claimer*, desperate yet sweet enough to marry a pregnant woman. In a weak moment Mary could've seen Jesus as the potential cause of her life being ruined by the threat of being stoned by the public, for instance. At that time and place, at least certain people in the neighbourhood most likely would've freaked out to see a pregnant woman wandering around displaying visual proof of having had casual sex out of wedlock. Given the circumstances, it's also quite possible that the *Claimer*, Joseph, might've been prone to abusing the kid he hadn't fathered. Or maybe after experiencing the miserable consequences of having given birth to a bastard son, the *Claimer* Mary could've been driven to the point of feeling the need to abuse someone weaker than herself, just like Sok's mom. And if Mary and Joseph had ended up having other sons together, they might've come to favour them over Jesus and treated him unfairly. Sok's already witnessed how orphans, beggars and the disabled in Korea in the 70s were treated. As it's a universal fact that in traditional cultures bastard children have been mistreated and ostracized, Sok doesn't see that when Jesus was growing up he would've been able to dodge the traumas caused by reactions from his own family and neighbouring community.

Another telling reflection on his *EM* inclinations is the compassion Jesus showed towards the persecuted whore, Mary Magdalene. Just as Sok was drawn to the beggar woman he saw as a child at the Lim clan's place where he was suffocated, Jesus must've felt compassion for Magdalene, most likely stemming from sharing the same kinds of traumas. Most probably they both felt unloved, supporting Sok's theory that Jesus might've also been abused and persecuted, much like this woman. Quite likely Jesus was a bastard who out of shared compassion hitched up with a whore with the altruistic intention of saving everyone, despite the equally speculative argument in *Jesus Christ Superstar* that Jesus had no such aspirations.

In order for Jesus to liberate people from the fear of death, he would've had to show that death is birth, like the transition of fetus-to-baby. The best way to do it would've been to demonstrate it physically, just as he did through his birth, crucifixion and resurrection. In addition, to overcome his traumas he accepted his death with no reaction and without selling out to save himself. Strikingly, Christianity has put a lot of emphasis on Jesus' birth through the celebration of Christmas, which Sok thinks is a fabrication of the church that bears little significance to the message of Jesus; rather, Sok would place more emphasis on Jesus' death and resurrection celebrated at Easter as being symbolic of the *unknown-trust cycle*. Nevertheless, despite Jesus' work, he wasn't able to liberate humanity from its fundamental fear of death, just as Buddha wasn't.

However, Sok also recognizes that Buddha and Jesus' apparent failures weren't necessarily the case, in the sense that from the beginning their intentions weren't meant to liberate anyone. Contrary to the common conception of them as liberators, Sok believes they came into the world as destroyers who quickened the movement of history towards doom. This is because over time as they were deified and worshipped as god-like figures, they became increasingly inaccessible. By elevating these idols to the level of unobtainable celestial beings, religious institutions constituted a hierarchical way of thinking that informed people's religious and spiritual lives to the degree that everyone felt, *There's someone hugely better than us!* Over the centuries, having such unattainable role models like Jesus and Buddha has created doubt, insecurity, dependency and destructiveness that have led to collective annihilation. That this shared response of submissiveness and self-limitation was expected by both Jesus and Buddha, while their work was to introduce a new *framework* of self-sufficiency, is apparent in their felt need for disciples to pass on their teachings. It must've been clear to them both that human beings weren't sufficiently evolved to be able to grasp the new *framework* they were initiating. People simply weren't ready to shake hands with kings and queens, let alone gods.

Since those times, people have remained in a state of denial as to the need to face the *unknown-trust cycle* that Buddha and Jesus tried to lead them into and enter the new *framework* that had been set out for them, like discovering a homework assignment that puts everyone into a condition of increased misery. Out of reaction to the burden of obtaining the state of *Triple Contrast* that Jesus and Buddha were already in, people wishfully started believing that these enlightened men would save them so they could continue procrastinating. This apathy initiated the rapid destructive decline all the way to now, and people are still reluctant to face the challenge of facing the *unknown* and death to enter into that new *framework* laid out so long ago by Jesus and Buddha.

At this crucial turning point of history, the chronic state of fear, denial and ennui in which people are trapped has to be corrected by the *Rider* in *Revelations*, a section of the *Bible* that has remained relatively intact, due to the fact that nobody's ever understood what the fuck it was talking about. The *Rider lifts the veil* to expose the existence of the new *framework* and allows humanity to realize its pending death. Viewed in this light, Buddha, Jesus and the *Rider* could be evil celestial agents because their existence, teachings and followings have pushed people closer to their doom or death to face the original *birth-death* dilemma. Sok views the influences of Jesus and Buddha as being neither good nor evil. They were merely *EM's* going about their work of quickening the world's doom, like bending what appears to be linear time into the circle of the *framework*. Everything comes to an end before it loops back towards a new beginning.

According to Sok, the era when Jesus was around was even worse than currently because people back then were completely behind in overcoming the concept of god, and therefore, were far from becoming choice makers. To bridge the gap, it was necessary for the human race to be brought a step further towards being conscious of the prospect of collective annihilation. In that regard, Jesus and Buddha did what they could to push everyone towards taking a ride on the Titanic. With the utmost enlightenment, clarity and emotional detachment, they chose what they thought was needed by offering themselves as examples of people who set no limits on what they were willing to do. In Sok's opinion that's love.

Thirteenth Canvas:
Quantum Theatre

1 I'm Not Sorry

Upon waking up to freedom Martyrs become Killers with their words without actually killing, while Killers become Martyrs who accept the feeling of being harassed without actually being harassed. This is the Quantum Theatre.

Sok conceives of the *Quantum Theatre* as a massive global role reversal, like a prince and a beggar exchanging roles, or the tale, *The Ant and the Grasshopper*. It's the climax before the end, designed to release everyone's pent up traumas and give them a slight sense of justice, like a real prince who's been playing a beggar finally getting his old self back. In addition to its cinematic entertainment value, the main purpose of the *Quantum Theatre* is to release traumas. The dilemma is that if a player acts out his reverse role in reality, rather than virtually, it'll generate another chain of traumas and reactions that will perpetuate the cycle of abuse and continuously have to be reversed. Although the reverse role is inherently illusive in that it's nonphysical in the sense that it's not like actually beating up a former abuser, it still requires an external act of words to release the trauma when a person's facing either his abuser or another fearful situation. Sok understands this is necessary to invite the *feeling* of the *unknown*, such as a person coming out with a secret about an organization or government, or saying a final farewell to his family or partner. Such acts open the door to an insecure tomorrow. Through his experience, Sok's found that in choosing his reverse role, his conscious choice to face the *unknown* of the future creates his new *framework*. This requires a leap of faith concerning future uncertainties. If the player doesn't realize the overall *framework*, he won't necessarily risk everything, whereas if he does have the *framework* in mind, he'll simply relax in the belief that the *unknown* is a new beginning that ends in trust.

Sok's noticed that playing his reverse role requires summoning a bit of reaction to his former self. For him it's about confronting and being confronted by the external action of coming clean about the past. The trauma has to surface first in order for him to face it with his words as ammunition. Sok deems that words are the portal between a person's internal and external realities. When everyone tells the truth, there's no more acting and the curtain drops. When there's no more need for a theatrical construct, all the players detach themselves from their past traumas to begin their new *framework*, like children with memories of acting out as grownups in the previous *framework*.

To begin the last act of the *Quantum Theatre* as *EM*, Sok initiates a domino effect by using his book as a medium for establishing his new roles as the *Rider* and writer. While playing his reverse role of *BFI*, he uses his words to bring to light the sum of everyone's traumas so they can face them, rather than continue to deny them. His strategy is to pass the traumas of history back onto *Martyrs*, who he knows are the most fed up and troubled of all the players. In the *Quantum Theatre*, when *Martyrs* receive from the *Rider* the new trauma that everyone's doomed, they risk their lives by withdrawing from all their dependencies to wake their own internal *EM* quality and play out their new external roles as *Killers*. He believes what makes them *Martyrs* in the first place is their lifelong avoidance of death, so that their acceptance of it in the *Quantum Theatre* turns them into *EMs* with no concept of tomorrow. Upon being awakened and emerging into their reverse roles they reveal secrets concerning what certain *Blamers* such as CEOs of multinational corporations have been up to, and in so doing, end up detaching themselves from *Blamer* activities. Along with *Martyrs*, mobs of *Claimers* (the majority of the general public) reveal every little secret they've been holding in about *Blamers* and their families so they no longer have to depend on them. Meanwhile, *Blamers* come out of the woodwork to accept full responsibility for their choices and actions by atoning for all the *Claimer* accusations and internalizing their reactions. In so doing, *Blamers* become *EMs* willing to be punished or die in recompense for past deeds.

In his *Quantum Theatre*, Sok imagines *Blamer*-types out on the street calmly accepting being pointed fingers at from the mob. By playing their new roles, *Blamers* and *Claimers* will finally get the chance to walk in each other's shoes. Like *EM*, in order to rebirth as a *Claimer*, each *Blamer* will for the first time experience the insecurity of tomorrow and witness the death of his egotistical old self. Equally satisfying for Sok will be watching *Claimers* rebirth into *EMs* by finally facing the feelings of insecurity they've been harbouring since birth, so that for the first time, they can experience not having anyone to depend on except themselves. Sok envisions the surfacing of many classy self-made male and female types pulling themselves out from their humble beginnings. As *Blamers* accept their losses, *Killers* will come clean, risking the potentiality of retaliation. Even if a person doesn't make it to the next *framework*, it's hugely beneficial to swim with the last minute surf, since it's the greatest opportunity to deal with his traumas to make his next existence easier. Sok explains that it's a much more difficult process for *Blamers* because their reverse role is naturally a more difficult one to accept. *BFI* finally plays the new *EM*, taking all the blame and heat he deserves from everyone to complete the *framework* of history. Ultimately all the self-chosen players become *EMs* by reclaiming their own inner child and returning to a paradise of their own creation, their own internal and external playgrounds where they're unfettered and free to play.

Sok muses that for everyone to start actualizing their reverse roles, *Blamers* such as CEO's of multinational corporations will need to live with a slight tilt towards the illusion of being good. Their purpose wouldn't actually be benevolence, but rather to hit a balance, as when riding an old misaligned bicycle, *Blamers* need to correct their tendency to lean towards one side of aggressively reacting. Therefore, by shifting slightly, *Blamers* can internalize other's verbal admonitions. Similarly, the *Claimer* majority needs to live with an opposite tilt towards entertaining the illusion of *breaking bad*. This will give them the satisfaction of waking themselves up to confront the pertinent issues in their lives instead of remaining in denial and merely fantasizing about what might've been.

Sok reminds himself that such specifics about playing reverse roles in the *Quantum Theatre* can simply be achieved by *Seeing Horses*. For *Blamers*, *Seeing Horses* means not reacting externally, since as they enter the realm of *Triple Contrast*, they lose the momentum of their emotional aggressions and internalize them. In the case of *Claimers*, *Seeing Horses* means waking themselves up just as they're habitually about to fall into daydreaming, so as to envision their external playground with a heightened intensity of *feeling*. Sok concludes that all the roles converge at the point of detachment. That's *Seeing Horses*.

Next is one of Sok's paintings, *I'm not sorry*, which he felt satisfied putting together as a visual expression of his words. It demonstrates how the *quantum* action of aiming language at his harassers extends to the realm of his paintings.

2 Scorpio's Sting

Sok's learned that his words are everything for playing out his reverse roles. Given his *EM* qualities, he's noticed people tend to become *Blamers* when they're around him, so gradually he's learned to activate his *Killer* side to return the aggression and pull himself out of his *Martyr* quandary. Often he's found he becomes a doormat until he comes to the clarity to strike back. His saving grace is he's a Scorpio with a sting. Even though he's always fundamentally rejected the idea of physical abuse, he's capable of casting stinging remarks with absolute candor and emotional detachment when he needs to. In such situations, he's learned to end one cycle of the *framework* with a person in a relationship or friendship so that he can move on. At such times, his words can be as cold as those of a murderer to stab the hearts of his listeners with the truth.

In one instance when Sok was in his early twenties, his dad committed suicide. Sok was in the apartment with him at the time. His dad sent his mom away on a false errand and proceeded to drink half a bottle of pesticide while Sok was in the other room. His sister had married a few months earlier and was at her new place, but Sok's always wondered why he was never sent away on some errand. Nevertheless, when Sok went into his parents' room to get something, his dad told him he'd drunk the pesticide, as if he were laying on a guilt trip. Looking back, Sok suspects that already his dad felt betrayed by his son, who'd been impatient with him for not killing himself sooner, considering his body was riddled with cancer, and he was suffering terribly. Upon entering his dad's room, Sok could see the bottle and smell the chemical on his dad's breath. He said, *Good!* and stormed back to his room.

With one word Sok had reversed his *Martyr* role of putting up with years of abuse to becoming an abuser-turned-*Killer*. As far as he was concerned his dad had chosen his own way out, and Sok was neither in the mood to act as if he could change anything nor engage emotionally, in which case he would've been expected to express his apologies and regrets over all his past exchanges with his dad. In keeping with the Lim family tradition of stark candor, however, that would've been acting and lies at the final grave moment between them, and he imagines his dad knew it. Sok accepted his dad's suicide as being the most reasonable solution, since after several cancer surgeries his dad didn't have any other solution but to drink cases of cough medicine to numb his pain. So as the next generation of the Lim clan, Sok thought it'd be his dad's dying wish that his son should at the last moment be candid and stand by his word. In Sok's mind, his dad had been responsible for years of falling into his own weak path of denial by not choosing an alternative. After exhausting all his options he'd chosen the same path of escape as he'd always done, procrastinating till the last minute until there was no alternative. But what Sok ended up appreciating most about his father was the fact that all his life his dad had clearly exercised his choice not to be a choice maker, and thereby given Sok the understanding of what it meant to make active choices in his life.

Ultimately it's not Sok's business to judge how his dad lived or died, but certainly it was his dad's own affair in his last breath to experience his life lesson. Sok's often felt for him in his darkest moments, brooding that in response to his own icy retort his dad might've died with a feeling of complete abandonment because he could've interpreted it as the ultimate Lim clan betrayal. At the moment of death, however, he might also have finally realized that all the blaming he'd done in his life was based on his inability to shirk off his dependencies, just as he'd been addicted to pharmaceuticals throughout his adult life. Sok's dad was an unsuccessful *Killer* with the acute potential of reversing his role and becoming *EM* as his life path, but Sok's grateful that his dad didn't succeed in order to give Sok the lessons he needed. Throughout his life his dad blamed everyone and everything, but in the end, *whom did he have left to blame except himself, especially since he was the one who finally killed himself?* Sok would like to believe that by committing suicide his dad finally completed the loop of the long Lim clan story of betrayal by taking responsibility for his own mess. Furthermore, Sok would hope that by playing his reverse role at the time of his dad's death, his father had a chance to atone for all the blaming he'd done, or as Jesus said, *Repent*, which Sok interprets as an act of taking responsibility. At any rate, the occasion marked the end of an agonizing misunderstanding his dad had generated over the years with everyone around him, especially Sok.

Sok doesn't remember how long he stayed in his room doing nothing about his dad. At some point his dad's sister and her husband dropped by. Sok pretended he didn't know anything about it, while at the same time being aware that as his dad was moving in and out of unconsciousness, he must have been witnessing his son's charade. But at the time, Sok thought that was his dad's problem because Sok was busy doing his best not to go to jail for murdering his father. Already prior to that occasion, the police had come to investigate his dad's report of being physically abused by Sok, when actually Sok had been trying to protect his mom from being beaten, either by throwing his dad down on the floor or stunning him with a slight punch in order to separate him from her.

It started one day while he was still in high school when Sok knocked his dad down with a punch while his dad was abusing his mom. Unfortunately Sok's aunt and her husband were on his dad's side, had already been clued in on Sok's physical interventions and had disapproved. With that track record, Sok knew he could easily become a scapegoat, but also throughout his life there'd always been that deeply engrained mistrust that no one would believe him, so at times he used to act dumb to minimize troubles. In the circumstances following his dad's suicide, he acted shocked and kept what he hadn't done for his dad to himself, while honestly he didn't really feel much of anything. Unfortunately he'd made the mistake of throwing the half empty bottle of pesticide away, which later on gave the police cause for suspicion. On top of that, the fact that his dad hadn't left any suicide note was further cause for police suspicion. Sok spent more than a few years wondering whether he'd been set up, especially considering his dad was a former CIA agent with extensive knowledge about law and criminology. In retrospect Sok often considers the fact that his dad waited to kill himself until he had only a couple of hundred dollars remaining to leave behind. In fact it seemed to Sok to be his dad's final statement, *Fuck you all!* Deep down Sok wanted to tell everyone that his dad had finally made his choice and done what he had to. But the *Victim/Saviour* in him knew he had to be careful, and so he continued to mistrust the words welling up inside him. Looking back Sok doesn't perceive any betrayal. He sees now that the real act of betrayal was the one Sok committed to himself for not having been ready to tell the truth to the police. In the end, he sabotaged himself for not actualizing his reverse role over his dad's suicide with the police and everyone else. On the other hand, it's also true that it wasn't yet time.

Throughout the three-day traditional Korean funeral, Sok was at the police station in Seoul being interrogated by two detectives who suspected him of foul play. From Sok's perspective, being locked up in prison for something he hadn't done somehow felt familiar, as if he were his revolutionary first uncle spending his high school years in prison for the crime of showing compassion for his people. However, being a parent *killer* is about the worst crime Koreans can imagine. Even so, wanting to avoid spending the rest of his life in prison and without yet having realized the power of his words, Sok put on a show for the detectives until his mom's wealthy sister came along, and through her lover, put pressure on the detectives to release him. He got out on the third and last day of the funeral. Sok reflects that whether or not he'd used his words with the Korean authorities would've been arbitrary to the decision as to whether he was released without grounds or locked up forever without a fair trial. Regardless, one midnight in winter on the same day as Sok's release, Sok and his family buried his dad in the mountain.

After his dad and sister's deaths, Sok hardly remembers anyone with whom he didn't end with a few words expressing his detachment. Nevertheless, he honoured his sister's last wish that her son, Sang, be able to come to Canada for a western education. A month before she passed away she asked Sok, who by then was fully established in Vancouver, to raise him. He gladly accepted. Sok's mom came along to look after Sang on a daily basis while Sok became their legal guardian, living with them on and off. During one of the longer periods that he lived with them in the North Vancouver home that Sok had arranged for Sang's dad to buy, Sok had decided to put all his energies into finishing his book. Getting close to what he thought was completion, though later it turned out not to be nearly as complete as he thought, he wondered, *After this, what then?* He thought that with the messiah twist no publishing house would give it the time of day. On top of that, it still had to be edited. Around that time, his nephew was attending high school and had been recommended by his school to an English tutor named Lee. As the months went by, gradually Sang and Lee became friends. In fact after Lee realized that Sang had been holding back information on the death of his mother, she found herself having become somewhat of a mother figure to him. At any rate, over a period of a couple of years while living in the North Vancouver house, Sok heard about Lee from his nephew and mother here and there.

Lee used to lecture in Asian Studies and Arts departments in three of Vancouver's universities but had found academia too stressful and discontinued, preferring to tutor fulltime in a dilapidated old RV in her driveway. Her true passion was performance in movement, costume, sound and words related to Japanese noh theatre. When she was a teenager, she'd played first violin in a symphony orchestra and participated in a modern dance troupe. After travelling around Europe and Asia, and living in Germany, she'd applied and been accepted into the English department at Cornell University. There she picked up her close reading and analysis skills, which later she developed as a method of probing more precisely and deeply into things. Gradually she focussed her interests into noh performance, learning noh dance, Japanese musical instruments and noh mask-carving, and producing noh-related films, as well as studying and eventually teaching Classical Japanese, which further deepened her training in literature, close reading and analysis. She felt it was the equivalent of the kind of focussed feeling she used to get growing up doing music, writing and dance. Like an archeologist, she'd subsequently spent several years delving into the nuances and meanings of ancient Japanese noh texts, as well as the death-related performance aspects of noh theatre.

When Sok met Lee, she was living in her North Vancouver home with her Korean husband, mom and son, already in his early twenties. The fact that she had a Korean husband on top of all her Asian and close reading and analysis background meant she might be someone who could communicate on the level of Sok's interests and possibly grasp his dystopian writing and painting. Despite the fact that she wasn't his fantasy woman, he felt irresistibly drawn to her because from their first meeting Sok felt she was the only one who'd ever had the patience and intelligence to listen to his intensely deep long loopy explanations. Over the years, he'd developed a way of talking and writing that tended to cram a lot of meaning into a few sentences, like poems, so as to get his point across and not to miss the rare chance to express himself. Ordinarily either people lost patience or simply didn't understand, but Lee did or at least tried.

Before they met, Sok had heard through his mom and Sang that Lee'd recently been diagnosed with breast cancer. Given his own dark past, he was intrigued. Presumptuously gathering everything he'd heard about her, Sok imagined her to be an over-worked, stressed out, dying woman. After Sok finished his revision, he thought he'd try to approach her to have a look at his book. Through Sang he contacted her, and she agreed to do an initial reading. Their very first meeting they hit it off. At that time, Sok didn't have any friends, and for more than a decade Lee hadn't really had anyone to talk to either. They met just before Christmas, a year after her cancer diagnosis, surgery and subsequent treatments. Sok's first impression meeting Lee was that she looked like a fifty-two-year-old woman recovering from cancer. She seemed exhausted but at the same time still possessed certain childlike aspects that Sok immediately recognized as typical *EM* qualities. On top of it, she had genuine sweetness, sparkling intelligence and some retarded, nerdy behavioural mannerisms that Sok had to admit he liked. Meanwhile, she was thinking Sok's next messiah thing in his manuscript was weird but nevertheless perceived a certain looping quality in his writing that went against conventional linear narrative structures. Lee played the crucial role as a friend to inspire Sok to develop a more concrete structure of the *framework*. In spending time with her, Sok felt the first real possibility of friendship, and after a short period they were inseparable companions, every day going for mountain and ocean walks while chattering endlessly about their uncanny similarities, pasts and mutual interests.

Oddly, between their North Vancouver homes, which ran parallel to each other, there was a wooden staircase that cut directly through a canyon and took about ten minutes to climb. One rainy night they had sex on that staircase. From then on they'd sneak around between his and her houses to be together. Like *Breaking Bad* (their favourite TV show, with the exception of *Dexter*), they were *EM*s playing their reverse roles, visiting motels and cabins, bringing cases of champagne, making love and talking for hours on end. On some level Sok had always envied people with cancer. He'd often dreamed of having it himself so that *Hedonist* and *Junkie/Addict* could just party for a month or two and then check out. Sok, with his wish for no tomorrow and need to escape the burden of the book, and Lee with her pent-up desires, became a fine team of destructive *EM*s, hiding, partying, conversing and lovemaking as often as they could. Soon it became their life focus. When Lee's family got to know about the affair she expressed her wish that they go their separate ways, and they all agreed.

By the time Sok was taking trips with Lee to escape and be together, his nephew, Sang, was ready to move to Quebec to go to university, and Sok's mom was preparing to sell the house and go back to Korea. At a certain point, the three of them only had a couple of months left before they went their separate ways. After Sang left, Sok and his mom became increasingly intolerant of each other, especially since Sok had recently introduced Lee into the picture. Before his mom first came to Canada, Sok had dreaded her arrival, and as a result, had initially let go of the idea of even having Sang come, because just around the time after *Seeing Horses* he thought he'd finally let go of his family. Obviously he hadn't, since he gave in when through his mom Sang's dad pleaded with

Sok to help out, and Sok weakly agreed, not knowing he'd have to pay big time over the next five years because of this decision.

While Sok was living in the North Vancouver house with his mom and nephew, his mom just assumed she was the decision maker. However, as Sang's guardian, Sok felt he had to counteract his mom, whom he felt was psychologically unsound and still suffering from postwar syndrome. Not only that, but she was living in a foreign country for the first time while for five years managing to maintain her stance of not speaking a word of English, right up until the end. Everything she did was exactly the opposite of what Sok would do, such as freely fumigating the inside of the house with deadly toxins, bleaching all the countertops, and with her son-in-law's approval, needlessly pumping the robust Sang full of antibiotics. Knowing this was exactly what his sister wouldn't have wanted, and that that was one of the reasons she'd chosen her brother to look after her son over both her husband and mother, Sok had many arguments with his mom as to how Sang should be brought up in Canada. To make matters worse, Sang would side with his grandmother saying, *What's the big deal about going on antibiotics?* By the time Sang was in grade ten, he'd become a spoiled little tyrant, ordering his Grandma around and playing computer games whenever he wasn't at school, in Lee's RV or at the gym channelling his masculine energies and pent-up anger through martial arts (an activity Sok had influenced him into).

Sang had lost his mother when he was in grade six, and prior to that had been abused and neglected by his parents. In addition, he'd been pushed too hard by his mom, who since he was born had been struggling with breast cancer and was concerned about the direction her son's life would take after she was gone. As Sok knew Sang had never dealt psychologically with any of his traumas, he felt his nephew could use some guidance. According to Sok's criteria, Sang was becoming a mass-murdering *Killer*, an exemplary *Blamer.* He came to the conclusion he'd have to play his reverse role in parenting his nephew, rather than being a friend to him as he'd always been in the past. So he detached himself from the relationship, like a mother bird kicking her chicks out of her nest when it's time for them to be independent. This wasn't easy because in a true sense, Sok had been Sang's only friend and parent ever since he was born. He'd always felt his bond with Sang to be similar to the one he'd had with his sister. Since Sang was a little boy, they'd been like best friends who communicated without any barriers. Sok had also always felt he was Sang's role model, his maternal uncle, guiding his nephew and freely sharing his unusual perceptions.

One of the most memorable exchanges between Sok and Sang occurred the night Sun died. Sang was asleep at home on his dad's request and as a result didn't witness the passing of his mother. Sok came back from the hospital and woke Sang up, calmly telling him, *Your mom died. I understand if you somehow don't feel so bad about her passing. If that's the case, cool.* Later Sang confessed that's exactly how he'd felt. From Sok's point of view, he'd never wanted Sang to feel the burden of having to act in front of him. Since Sang's birth the bond between them had always been strong.

Nevertheless, Sok began cutting off the emotional tie between them, even though he had a hard time withdrawing. Whenever Sang laughed, Sok could hear his sister's laughter. But in order to make sure Sang got what he needed, Sok detached even to the degree that it would be fine with him if they never saw each other again. Since then Sok's respected Sang's choice to continue to remain financially dependent on his father in order to attend the top business school in the country to please his dad. Even though he knows that so far Sang has only suppressed his traumas, he trusts his nephew will learn from his choices and that's his business. In the end, Sok's left with the comfort of knowing that in his reverse role he became a stranger to his nephew in order to give him a chance to trust in himself without having any dependency, expecting that once they departed they'd possibly never see each other again.

After living several years together in Canada, Sok and his mom also came to the conclusion they didn't want to continue their relationship. Sok's mom was acting as if she'd completely had it, while Sok was doing the same. They often yelled at each other over trivial matters. In one of these exchanges when Sok became so frustrated he started swearing at her, she pushed him. With a reflexive action he pushed her back, and she fell. At that moment, Sok knew that if there were ever a time to kill his mom it was then. Towards the end of the period they lived together, his killing urge had elevated to an unprecedented level so that sometimes he had to moan in his room or stab a tree in their yard over and over with a knife until he was exhausted to prevent himself from acting on his impulses. If he'd allowed *Killer* to have his way, he'd have stabbed her many times, but his other characters thought differently. Still he had to do something, so instead of killing her he poured some water in her ear and then immediately left the house and his entire family situation behind him to go live in a motel. Although Sok wasn't proud of what he'd done, through the incident he came full circle to face his initial abuser and the origin of his trauma. In retrospect, by facing the chance of returning the abuse to his abuser, he'd arrived at a crossroads between becoming the murderer he'd always thought he was, perpetuating the cycle of Cain and being forever stuck in his reversed role, or disengaging as best he could, however blundering an attempt it turned out to be. The instant he made the latter choice, he freed himself.

A month after the incident with his mom, Sok moved out of the motel and into Lee's place. During the three months he lived there he worked full time renovating and helping Lee get her house ready to be put up for sale. Gradually he started to feel trapped by Lee's dependency on him to help her get the house ready, while he wasn't able to spare even an hour to finish his book. In the past when this kind of doubt had started creeping in, it invariably meant ending the relationship. He'd never found a way to bypass this problem because employing his reverse role in his relationships with women by detaching from the situation had never worked out. Although he was devastated at the thought of losing Lee, he simply didn't know how else to go about changing his circumstances. He knew that if he didn't disengage himself, he'd always harbour doubts about her, and their association would eventually end in disaster anyway. It was true that Lee had been a friend, someone with whom he thought he'd come the closest to everything he'd ever wanted, but he found himself caught in her extremely challenging life situation with the dream of his book gone totally out of the picture. So Sok moved out after doing everything he could to make the house beautiful. During what was for the most part a three-month lockup in his new North Van apartment, Sok focused on rewriting the book he'd been sorely neglecting.

What Sok had to clarify was whether Lee would still be able to maintain her friendship with him, even if it meant letting him go. This need came from the Lim clan's revolutionary tradition of withdrawing from ambiguous friendships that could potentially turn into betrayals, a scenario that's always deadly in any kind of revolution. In the past he'd experienced that when it came down to the final crunch, people would either do anything to protect themselves or else cling to a relationship over a friendship. But in Sok's opinion, there isn't any chance for love or friendship when people aren't willing to let go to acknowledge the other person's desire to pursue his or her personal interests. Out of fear of losing their loved ones, people can become quite controlling. According to Sok, being able to say goodbye with a feeling of detachment is the most important quality of friendship, but Sok had started to doubt Lee on that note.

After moving out of Lee's place, on one of the days she visited Sok in his apartment, he told her about his doubts concerning their friendship. Due to their eight-year age difference, he'd also started to feel her family suspected him of going after the house money. Sensing potential complications brewing in her family over the house, Sok suggested Lee consider playing her reverse role by walking out empty-handed from her situation and coming to live with him. At that time, Sok felt particularly impatient about finding a level of freedom away from family attachments now that he no longer had his mom around. As Lee had already experienced the ways in which Sok had acted on his doubts before, she knew he meant every word. Given her debt burden, even with the bit of money Sok had left, they practically wouldn't have anything. Considering Lee's bout with cancer, it must've seemed like falling into an *unknown* abyss, as suicidal as jumping off a tall building. Nevertheless, within an hour Lee had made up her mind. She agreed to hand over her portion of the house and walk out. Sok was impressed that Lee was an *EM* as crazy as him.

As Sok spent more time brooding in his solitary lockup, he came to realize he'd been controlling Lee like a puppet because he knew she'd do anything to keep the relationship. It occurred to him that the person Lee really might need to be free from was Sok. By remaining involved with her, he might be robbing her of the opportunity to stand alone, after spending so many years living in a stifling co-dependent environment. He thought her decision to free herself from everyone should be for herself, rather than for Sok or the relationship. It also occurred to him that having her in his life might be taking away from his own experience of facing the *unknown*. With his mom finally out of his life he wanted to experience the rebirth of becoming *BFI* by facing the world alone without any doubts or insecurities. On top of it all, he worried there might be a conflict of interest in their relationship, based on his speculation that Lee's working with him on his book might be a factor in what was alluring him to her. In that sense, remaining involved with her might be diluting his own experience of facing the *unknown* by being dependent on someone. He wanted his rebirthing to be a graceful one full of pure trust in the *unknown*, void of future-oriented worries about how to edit and publish the book, what to do with Lee or deal with his new life.

After all those considerations, Sok informed Lee that he wanted to break up. She didn't take it very well but offered to help him with the book purely as a friend. Sok refused on the grounds that he'd decided he just didn't want to see her at all. Although he knew he'd need editing at some point, he thought it would be interesting to see how things came to him all on their own if he just *allowed* them to. Instead of imagining any particular future *Point B* regarding the book or Lee, everyday he focussed only on writing, eating and sleeping. Just like Alice in *Wonderland*, Sok had once again come full circle by locking himself up without any friends and little money. The difference this time was that he felt utterly at ease and got to know himself better.

Sok sees anyone who comes into his life as an opportunity to let go of his old traumas so he can start his new *framework* trauma-free; on the other hand, he knows the risks of dealing with traumas. In order for him to come to terms with and accept any of his past ordeals, he's had to confront them first, which means reentering that past state and making traumas real again. That entails being re-traumatized to a certain degree. Sok's learned that the sign of a trauma being revisited is when he becomes so engaged he's unable to detach from his emotional reaction. When he's so overcome by emotion he becomes irrational, takes everything personally and is in danger of losing himself in perpetual reactions upon reactions. Once Sok engages emotionally in a trauma, there's a chance he can lose sight of what he's doing and why. Only when he's in a calm state of emotional detachment can he view the situation from a third-person point of view.

When a person gains certain objectivity, he can begin to move away from the old trauma. Sok interprets the entire process of falling into traumas and detaching from them as love in the circular movement of the *unknown-trust cycle*. As much as love is detachment, an initial emotional reaction is always necessary to get it going. For instance, when Sok's mom was finally able to accept Sok's detachment and disengage emotionally from him in her phone call from the airport, or when Sok's dad was confronted with Sok's detachment and was forced to accept it during his last moments, both were experiencing the death of their old selves that they'd long been stuck with because of their inability to face their traumas. Therefore, when Sok created these dramas by playing his reverse role, stirring up deeply rooted traumas and then disengaging, his parents also reached the end of their cycles, experiencing the completion of their age-old *frameworks* and their manifestations of new ones. According to Sok, *allowing* and detachment are the same in the sense that *allowing* doesn't permit any action based on emotion. But *allowing* implies that what was *allowed* actually comes. *Allowing* is love, and love is creation.

Although it's always risky to re-involve oneself in past emotional traumas, over the years Sok's become an expert at finding ways to detach, regardless of how reactive he's become within the dramas he creates. Since he's the most suspicious guy, he inevitably comes to the point of doubting himself, usually while he's in full reaction mode. With that understanding he acknowledges his mother for having given him the most amazing gift of self-doubt, like a nutritious care package. One day Sok visited his mom from Lee's place before he moved into his apartment. He told her it must've been difficult living with such a paranoid son, and that her life could've been easier if Sok, his sister and their dad had been more like the kind of Koreans she could relate to. With a final deep appreciation of her, at the age of forty-four Sok severed the umbilical cord.

Throughout his life, Sok's *framework* of engagement and detachment has been what's occupied him with his own family, relationships and everyone else. As family traumas are the most fundamental, it took a long time for his family to complete the cycle. But during the process, gradually Sok got wiser at detecting patterns. Although the people in the past with whom Sok played are all gone, and he's finally left alone in the world, Sok's felt the desire to detach even further. He's come to recognize the pattern of needing to disengage from everyone and everything out of love to finish one cycle. As *EM*, in order to detach himself in his reverse role, Sok started systematically disengaging. Ultimately he felt the need to put everything he had to say into one book to detach from everyone and everything. That's been the purpose of his writing. Nevertheless, what Sok hadn't realized until recently was that at some point, he needed to detach himself from the writing he'd been so obsessed with over the last seven years!

3 Deer Caught in a Headlight

One day after the breakup with Lee as his work was getting closer to being done, Sok was writing about role reversal. He'd been moving in and out of being the detached observer, watching himself writing with passion and devotion as he always did, while putting everything else that constituted his life on the back burner. Sequestered in his apartment, his intention was that this time he wouldn't come out until he'd really finished. But he'd also begun to see that in the past his lockup stunt had never worked out, and that was why to this day he was alone still writing. Even so, he knew that it was something he had to do once and for all, and was ready to sacrifice anything to achieve it. Underlying everything were lurking doubts as to whether the book would ever go anywhere. If that were the case, he wondered if he should just keep on trying indefinitely. In that moment of self-reflection, Sok saw himself with his stubborn self-destructive masculine drive forever chasing a rainbow. He understood then that his obsessive ambition finally to make something of himself ultimately stemmed from his self-doubt. It was *Sabotager/Destroyer* in action, the self-betrayer in him always making sure he sabotaged himself so completely that whatever revolution he launched would never work out, and he could confirm everyone's expectations, especially his parent's, that he was a loser. It meant that where the book was concerned, Sok couldn't see there might be a reverse role he needed to apply. Suddenly Sok realized the remaining trauma he still hadn't faced was the necessity to finish the book so that at long last he could put to rest all the original traumas it had caused to resurface.

Sok began to apply the same reasoning to his messiah belief. As the very conception of wanting to become a messiah stems from being *EM* and necessarily means letting go of everyone and everything, he suddenly found himself questioning why he'd never thought to challenge his messiah conviction in its reverse role. He finally saw how oblivious he'd been to a corner of himself he'd never confronted because it'd been so central to his desperate attempts to rescue himself, while promising the added satisfaction of being able to justify meddling in other people's lives. His messiah dream, which he started to see had evolved out of his childhood fantasy of being a superhero, meant that not only had he been interested in saving himself, but he had also found it important to be able to affect the lives of others on a global basis in order to attain the recognition he was seeking. He'd been willing to give up his life for the cause, but *when had he ever thought about letting go of the old tired-out belief about being the next messiah?* The epiphany had a shocking resonance Sok couldn't deny, like a deer caught in a headlight.

As he probed further into this insight, he reflected on his history of breaking up with women. He wouldn't necessarily have repeatedly done it unless he was waiting for a certain aspect of the present to be changed in the future. He wondered, *Then why had it been even necessary to break up with Lee, as if I didn't want her? How could having her in my life change my striving for the **unknown**, if everyday with her was already an **unknown**? Where is the trust if I'm unable to **allow** Lee in my life?* For years he'd been blinded to the fact that as long as he continued to doubt, he'd always need a person like his mother to sustain his old need to play his reverse role because that way he could play his mom's reverse role. His past antagonists were a mirror image of himself; they worked together to propagate the codependency of abuser and abused. All along it had been him choosing to manipulate his relationships by always suspecting other people of validating his own mistrust in them. He justified his stance, yet the truth was that, *If there were anyone who knew how to let go of doubt it'd be him because of **Seeing***

Horses, which instantaneously brings everything down to the visceral level. During his last lockup, it became clear to Sok that he'd been neglecting his own power.

With this new understanding, Sok knew it had been necessary to break up with Lee and create all the other sagas in his life, since without them he wouldn't have been able to come to see that he was the director and producer of his own dramas. To put this new understanding into effect, he's had to let go of his old role of *Victim/Saviour*, the persona underlying his desire to play messiah, and the one who would've done anything to convince Sok to continue playing. On the other side of Sok's psychological spectrum, like a drill sergeant, *Warrior* had deemed it only possible to finish the book if Sok faced the *unknown*. After all, it was Sok's *EM* propensity towards self-denial that had initially prompted him to travel a certain route to be qualified to become a messiah, so much so that recently he'd been worrying he'd lose his self-devotional purity by allowing himself to be with Lee. In terms of the book, due to his extreme insecurity he'd originally wanted to turn everyone else on the planet into the opposite of himself so that he could play out his fantasy of being saviour, while the rest of the world would become victims in need of being saved. That way he'd be able to imagine he was no longer in trouble and everyone else was. In the process he'd constantly condemned everyone else as being helpless sufferers in order to satisfy himself emotionally by perpetuating his game of being saviour versus everyone else playing victim.

Sok's never felt free in his old role of messiah—the role of not trusting anyone—since deep down it had always made sense to him that his past was laid out to be a messiah so he might have the chance to go against everyone he couldn't trust. Just as from a historical perspective, in their reverse roles kings and queens would be at the bottom of humanity's heap, choosing to play the messiah would be the equivalent of deciding to be the most unfree man in relation to everyone else. Sok's realized he doesn't ever want to play that role again. He's no longer anyone's messiah and just wants to live the rest of his life as a normal person doing fun things with Lee. Maybe she'll edit, and they'll publish the book together with the aim of becoming self-sufficient in an apocalyptic world. *Who even needs* **Seeing Horses** *when Sok and Lee's sex goes deeper than anything?* After letting go of the role of playing messiah, Sok no longer feels the need for recognition. He knows now he should just work with what he's got.

Sok doesn't have any more roles to reverse. The last one he's given up is becoming a messiah. It was the most retarded role, but it was the one that saved him because otherwise he'd never have been able to maintain his self-esteem throughout the many years of struggling to return to his original self. From now on, he's his own messiah. In that sense, he's saved himself and succeeded in manifesting his own self-revolution.

4 National Prototypes

Out of [the Rider's] mouth comes a sharp sword with which to strike down the nations. "He will rule them with an iron scepter." He treads the winepress of the fury of the wrath of God Almighty.

Revelation 19:15

In order to play his reverse role, Sok had to put himself in the shoes of his abusers to see himself through the *Blamer/Claimer* matrix. Now he sees his reverse role as a shadow of his past, which only became old when he began emerging into his new *framework* and finally came to see what he'd been doing all his life. To play his reverse role he took the illusive action of letting go of his past and moving into the *Quantum Theatre* where his reverse role played itself out in the mirror image of his old role. However, an external playing out of his reverse role as real action is no different from his old role. For instance, a rapist might be someone who hasn't been able to get a person to love him in reality because he has rapist written all over his insecure expression, which irks an instantaneous reaction in women to reject him outright. Those women were likely also to have been rejected in the past, and therefore, have a desire to be the ones to reject this time. What the rapist wants is to witness his victim's humiliation as she's being violated. While he's raping her, he sees his own face in her expression as a kid going through the trauma of rejection, and so he feels he's not alone. However, in his false reverse role of acting as a rapist, he becomes an abuser who chose to play his reverse role as abused later. Instead, he'd have to go through role reversal in the *Quantum Theatre* to be done with playing any more roles. The *Rider* emphasizes that having to be abused later by choosing to abuse this time is not some kind of cosmic justice system punishing someone's wrong act; rather, it's simply a matter of a person making a choice to manifest his reality to create a chance to be in the abuser or victim's shoes so he can see and embrace himself by accepting either one without any reaction. He initiates a ping-pong rally of constant switching between the roles of abuser and abused until he drops the ball. By going through such a process, at long last he's able to detach from acting in both his old and reverse roles to reach the point of no more acting. To achieve that degree of detachment he frees himself of his past traumas so he can live like a child again without the emotional burden of wanting revenge or success.

Sok's found one of the easiest ways for a person to gain perspective of his old role is to reflect on his national characteristics. Nations and countries are the geographical and collective outcome of human reactions over time. If a typical countryman possesses these shared national characteristics, he'll likely never question his role and will continue to sit on top of accumulative individual and collective reactions within the mould of his particular national cookie cutter. Sok imagines each country as a macrocosm of a person that can be categorized stereotypically as either a *Blamer* or *Claimer* nation. This filters down to the personal level in that individual citizens can take on corresponding *Blamer* or *Claimer* characteristics. The *Rider*'s observed that generally speaking, leading nations infuse their citizens with the qualities of *Blamers*, while on the opposite end of the spectrum there are the countries made up of individuals playing out *Claimer* and *Martyr* traumas that still haven't emerged from a national sense of being victimized.

The *Rider* speculates that if all the nations on the planet were to be viewed as an individual, they'd seem like a bunch of kids playing at recess, bullying and being bullied in as colourful a psychological array as is humanly possible. In that sense nations and schools are mini-societies in which there's no nation or kid that doesn't hate some other nation or kid, and their alliances and disputes are constantly changing. In response to their traumas, all are competing to find a comfortable position or impose power over each other. The *Rider*'s observed that over the centuries, even the poorer, less powerful nations cling to certain glorious moments in their histories to evoke national pride with the economic or military dream of becoming a superpower one day, just as that nation's individual citizens are constantly vying for money, power and fame within their own daily lives. Nevertheless, before nations are able to switch their roles, they collectively generate a patriotic feeling of victimization to protect themselves. Depending on the level of national antagonism, they might react through an aggressive false reverse role or opt for a more passive-aggressive route.

Among the passive-aggressive nationalistic reactions, the most fundamentalist is: *We're God's chosen nation.* This is the same as saying, *As you've been fucked up at birth because you're not us, what's the point of your existence?* This attitude of contempt causes those self-claimed chosen nations to become dependent on everyone else being doomed at some point. When this insult to other nations happens, it becomes quite impossible for so-called non-chosen nations to tolerate the God-chosen nations, so from this point on it becomes a mutual reaction on both sides to lock into a codependency between abuser and abused.

On the other hand, if people in so-called chosen nations really believe they've been chosen by God, they won't mind being hated by less fortunate nations since that condition will be only temporary. Just as a prince in a beggar's outfit wouldn't necessarily mind being taunted, since he knows who he really is and where he'll return, there's no reason the self-proclaimed chosen nation should react defensively. So then the question becomes: *If it's not true they've been chosen, why in the world would they choose to play the role of being hated and persecuted?* The *Rider* wouldn't feel sympathetic towards the occurrence of historical atrocities, knowing the harassed individuals and nations willingly chose to remain in a state of dependency with and adoration of their harassers (their role models), so much so that they become harassers themselves at some point. So according to the law of choices, they're just perpetuating the choice of being abused repeatedly.

Once there are God's chosen nations, other nations react by wanting to be superior. The *Rider* thinks that on the human stage everyone's free to react no matter whether they think they're a nation chosen by God or one that believes its superior enough to conquer God's chosen nations. When it comes to superiority and national pride, there's no exemption because every nation flaunts its flags and anthems. But just as everyone can't be superior all at once, conflict and war are inevitable. From the *Rider*'s perspective, *If everyone's interested in superiority, how can anyone vilify dictators like Hitler and Napolean Bonaparte, who happened to be the coaches who everybody blamed in the team sport that everyone agreed to play?*

Among the superpower nations, the United States has been the one everyone would kill to play. It's been the smartest *Blamer* in actualizing what everyone else has been pursuing. To some, the US could be viewed as being a somewhat emotionlessly detached player in the game of *Monopoly*, unlike other superpowers that have disqualified themselves with their emotional need to win. As being on top requires that everyone else be underneath, people of dominant nations have been the most dependent in the sense that they've needed everyone else to uphold their position by being their servants. However, behind the American reign of prosperity the question looms: *What's the reverse role of a king who's been dethroned?*

For some time, certain European countries have been selling their cultural superiority in the areas of food, language and art, since they like to lay emphasis on their seniority over the rest of the western world because they've never been able to claim military and financial power over Americans, or recently, anyone else for that matter. But the *Rider* would like to challenge them to contemplate the reverse role of their cultural superiority by suggesting they first go to the Himalayas and try to live with a couple of goats, a few tea leaves and some dry dung, and while in utter seclusion with little oxygen and no admiring audience still pull out the spread they've been flaunting with their superior languages and hand gestures waving like a conductor.

It's clear that although none of the super nations would ever willingly choose to experience its reverse role, the *Rider* claims it's inevitable because of the future-orientation of the global economy. Its continuation thrives on the hope of tomorrow, which is people's justification for going into debt today. In order for nations and individuals not to have to pay back their debts, which in most cases exceed their assets, individual and national growth have to be ongoing to rationalize present day spending beyond everyone's means. But the planet's resources aren't being sustained in proportion to global population growth or industrial, scientific and technological development. Some might argue that all the world's natural resources are inexhaustible, since they can be combined, decomposed and combined again into various forms and products. The *Rider's* comment on that is: *That'd only be true if the process of artificially combining and decomposing took the same amount of time as the natural cycle. So why do human beings make things that take thousands or millions years to decompose? If a six-pack plastic ring kills the last bird, how much would it cost to make a bird?* As an aside, the *Rider* adds that with deadly plutonium waste on the rise that no one has any clue how to deal with, humans are playing their reverse role of being insects, germs and weeds.

The *Rider* submits that when it comes to nations hating one another, it doesn't only end with borderlines. It also extends to ethnic divisions. The eagerness of certain ethnic groups to step on each other has sometimes been taken to the extreme: *We'll finally be able to live happily when you all go away, and there'll be no more chance of your avenging us!* The basis of their choice is sheer hatred, which they usually effectively communicate through extreme aggression. It seems no other justification's necessary. Furthermore, killing absolutely everyone's crucial since they know their abhorrence will be avenged if they don't. The *Rider* sees that their reverse role is to be despised for no reason since they've killed for no reason.

The extension of being hated is similar to a sense of being rejected by fate, luck, god or cosmic forces. The *Rider's* watched peoples after peoples being born and born again only to become victims of various natural and manmade disasters. However, he ventures to intervene by suggesting that nothing's coincidence and everything's manmade in that it's a consequence of choice. Just as targets of ethnic cleansing feel victimized for no reason, aggressors playing their reverse roles have to realize that their being victimized in unexplained natural disaster, famine and disease is a consequence of their choice in the karmic sense that if those harassers died and came back, they'd experience some kind of karmic consequence of feeling unfairly victimized by forces out of their control such as a natural disaster. *Ultimately whose choice is it?* The question the *Rider* asks is: *Are they that invincible in the face of the boomerang they've thrown?*

The dominant superpowers aren't the only nations breeding hostility. The *Rider's* observed that passive-aggressive nations also spawn a lot of victims by creating subtler, yet in some ways more pervasive traumas. It's like a disagreeable, rude person who'll ruin the day for a hundred thousand people during the course of his lifetime. Koreans, in particular, specialize in ruining the day for each other three-hundred-sixty-five-days of the year. There's no Korean who doesn't loathe other Koreans in his daily exchanges of aggression or passive-aggression, expressing his self-created miseries through external factors such as family betrayal, society, luck, fate or the provocation of other nations, while at the same time remaining complacent in his belief that he's being loyal to family and country, and would never betray anyone. When Koreans do betray each other, they defend themselves on traditional or cultural grounds, imagining such arguments justify their harassment of the weak that extends to their children and pets. On that note, the *Rider* raises the challenge, *Is it coincidence that Koreans have their notorious dog soup?*

The country for which Sok feels the most compassion is North Korea because he relates his own traumatized South Korean upbringing to the individual lives of North Koreans. A child born in the North will often be taken away from his parents to be brainwashed by his godhead, who he knows will kill him or condemn him to a life of labour in the mines at any hint of rebellion. Based on his own experience, Sok believes that North Koreans don't even have the concept of freedom within their mental space. From birth, not only don't they have anything to eat, but more devastatingly, they can't even trust their parents, neighbours or friends, who won't hesitate to rat on them for their minimal survival. As there's no such thing as North Koreans being able to exchange feelings concerning their incessantly imminent fear of death, they remain trapped within their psychological state with no chance of release. Throughout their lifelong misery, all they can wish for in taking on their reverse role is to return or pass on their traumas to someone else. From their point of view, there's nothing and no one they wouldn't blame for their suffering, and so they want to take revenge by killing anyone without discrimination on an instant's notice when ordered to do so by their leader. The *Rider* submits that many of them would like nothing more than to engage in mass murder the first chance they get. He knows from his own self-probing that they must feel such an irresistible attraction to self-annihilation to end their misery that they've become monster soldiers. The *Rider* doubts whether North Koreans will be able to get a grip on their collective killing urge in the short time remaining, while it's taken Sok half a lifetime to process his. Therefore, he predicts that in the near future, they'll more likely resume the Korean War that's been dormant ever since the truce, out of their attraction to carry on the role of family betrayal between North and South they've been stuck for half a century playing. As it seems Koreans are never able to break out of their victim roles, the *Rider* foresees they'll cast themselves repeatedly into the role of victims of outrage.

Another example of a *Martyr* country like South Korea is India. Most East Indians accept the caste system that allows for a group of people called the untouchables to act as scapegoats for other Indians to dump their traumas onto the weak, so they can rise above their basic feelings of insecurity stemming from their challenging reality. The majority of the Indian population's set itself up as a bully at the expense of a most poverty-stricken minority that's never had a hope of fighting back. The *Rider* sees that Indians who accept the caste system within their own country assess all other human beings in terms of whether they're lower or higher ranking. This unpleasant tendency of Indians to judge everyone else according to their own hierarchical mindset causes other people and nations all over the world to react with an attitude of pure racism by treating Indians as the world's untouchables. Therefore, anyone who views someone else as an untouchable is the equivalent of being an untouchable himself.

The *Rider* sees that India and other holy countries have been practising seeing the emperor's clothes jeering, *He has a beautiful garment!* to backpacking western untouchables who upon return to their home countries can be found everywhere chanting, *Since I've been in India I'm holier than you, but not as holy as cows and rats.* The *Rider* inquires, *If holiness and sacredness are real, then why don't children know about them? At what age do people start taking an interest in holiness or sacredness anyway? And who makes the decisions as to what's holy and what's isn't? Indians?*

The *Rider* views China as a super shining car, bigger than a Hummer on the world stage but held up by children and old ladies underneath. China makes movies featuring serious-faced Kung Fu guys who magically fly around revealing their emotional need for power and recognition on an unimaginable scale. Their efforts to prove themselves in every field to a humanly impossible proportion are almost as dazzling as the fans of male peacocks. But the *Rider* wonders, *Don't they see their tricks don't impress girls in other nations enough to throw themselves on Chinese males and replenish all the baby girls killed in accordance with the one baby policy? What would be enough to quell the energies of all those womanless, young, horny males with their masculine drive to be **Blamers**? Interested as it was in being involved in the Korean War before the truce between North and South Korea, is China ready to have another arm wrestle with the US?*

The *Rider* understands that China's the superpower that's been giving everything it's got to reclaiming the supreme status it had in ancient times, even if it means obtaining it at the finishing line of the arm's race of human history. Like the Japanese national flag that symbolizes the Japanese conception that they're at the centre of the world, China 中国 also means "country at the centre." This ingrained Asian ambition, combined with the as yet unleashed power of China's massive population, makes it the last, yet scariest, most intimidating superpower.

The *Rider* would classify Canada as a *Blamer* nation. Its citizens patronize both *Blamer* and *Claimer* nations with their annoying Canadian flags on their backpacks, along with their wholesome political correctness, habit of killing the party mood and convenient discounting of the fact that they are one of the worst nations environmentally, even worse than the US. The Canadian tendency towards passive-aggression as a concept of justice, by acting like polite, caring human beings who denounce seemingly non-caring human beings, masks their deep-seated inner depression of not being able to play out their reverse role of throwing a temper tantrum whenever they want to and creates the gloomy society they rave about. But the *Rider* asks, *Who were they in their former role to deserve the great country they rave about?*

The Japanese have never been passive. This stems from their isolated island setting, which one would think would make it difficult for them not to be passive when it comes to interacting with the rest of the world. However, out of their reaction to living in paradisal seclusion, they've often decided to take action to attack first, imagining there's Japan and the rest of the world that'll eventually invade them at some point. This is opposite to Koreans who are forever waiting for their peninsula to be invaded. Japanese have the capacity, fierce dedication and intelligence to die or suffer for their country and culture. This comes from their attraction to death, which gives them their scary edge underneath all their polite interactions. The *Rider* sees that Japanese actions over conflicts of interest with other nations make them invite international and internal disasters such as falling nuclear bombs or their recent nuclear power plant disaster, so that they can feel they're melting down the tiny fragment of land they're standing on. The *Rider* ponders, *But who's going to suffer most when there are no more fish?* The Japanese are their own worst enemies that they have to overcome. The *Rider* adds that since they didn't seal up their nuclear leak right away and months later still haven't, *Can they complain about a guy who's going to fumigate himself in a jam-packed elevator?*

The *Rider* hears Mexicans reciting, *Gringos did this and Gringos did that!* In their view, Gringos have hindered Mexican success. The query the *Rider* confronts them with is this: *If they become successful in the future, they won't be able to say Gringos ruined them, and therefore, contradict themselves after having become successful. Who's ruining who?*

Besides nations, there are subgroups of people in professional categories or cultural groups all over the planet who share the same reactive patterns. For instance, some *Claimers* who feel they should just be given a free ride react by playing the roles of saviours or heroes of the planet. They often become artist wannabe's, activists or spiritual leaders who set themselves up as tollbooths and charge for giving directions to where they've never been. Or else under the name of charity, they break the wings of others by creating dependency. The *Rider* views such pretentious people as reacting on their pasts by being devoted to saving the planet with their fundraisers, songs, programs and public gatherings. Their reverse role would be to become *EM*'s by accepting responsibility for their own well-being and self-sufficiency, instead of blaming others for inaction, wrong action or lack of compassion. Ultimately these *Claimers* generate hope instead of doom, which doesn't sell. The *Rider* comments, *Without absolutely understanding the collective aim of human beings, how can they know their actions are even helpful to other people, animals, the environment or the planet? So what are they doing soliciting for their cause? Isn't it really all about helping themselves?*

Another group of domineering *Claimers* reacting on feelings of rejection are the meditating, hybrid-driving, yoga mat-carrying New Agers. The *Rider* sees that their old role is to assume the privilege of living in leisure and inaction on the basis that they're the chosen ones backed by the universe. In their thought bubble they muse: *I don't believe in God, and therefore, I'm free from him, so I must have been chosen by the universe, which means I'm privileged to be automatically free.* As far as the *Rider's* concerned, they aren't any different from many Christians selling mannerisms instead of love. In actuality their old role is one of inaction and pure dependency, which would chart their reverse role to be one of pure action. But the *Rider* detects a problem: *Won't they disappear once they assume their reverse role? What's the reverse role of non-action in the* **Quantum Theatre**, *since unfortunately, there are no real actions in a theatre based only on words?*

The *Rider's* observed that Christians have a need either to convert others to their point of view or decide how other people should live, like controlling parents deciding their kids' future. Considering that when people choose to be Christian they submit to allowing God to make their decisions for them in order to dodge responsibility and indulge in non-action, their reverse role would be to become independent choice makers who abandon their previous lives and go on a quest to find out whether or not it's God or themselves who's determining their fate. *Too late maybe?* the *Rider* gibes, reflecting that getting over traumas takes as much time as regaining health after a lifelong illness. The only reverse role Christians would want is to play God. But the *Rider* points out that in the *Quantum Theatre* that role doesn't exist.

If a person acts on the urge to kill someone else knowing it was too late to reverse his role, what this action means at the end of the world and the beginning of a new *framework* is that he's decided to follow the route of Cain. If that's his choice, like Sok, he'll go through the old *framework* of the whole of human history being hated and persecuted for seemingly no reason in order to learn about the consequences of murder. That's something Sok'd never want to repeat. He's learned his lesson.

Having almost come to his last words, the *Rider* points out that the only way for any person to attain freedom is to choose to be free. But only a freeman would know that from his experience. If he's free, he chose to be so and has learned how to make a choice to become a choice maker. In his new perception, he sees that everything, including all of the traumatic incidents in his life, had to happen as a matter of his choice. That logical circle is the *framework*. After the freeman has already entered into the new *framework*, he also knows that the conclusion of the entire *framework* means the inevitable end, and that so far, he's the only one who's recognized it as anything other than speculation. The freeman chooses to write about the *framework* and the end, since a freeman doesn't have any secrets. *Why would he?*

In his book, Sok writes about the end of the world. Understanding what he has to say can give a person temporary 3-D enlightenment. In his writing he freely expresses whatever he feels like saying. He does it by proclaiming freely how everyone else is utterly unfree while he feels ridiculously free. Like the kid in the *Emperor's New Clothes*, *EM* has nothing to fear. Now what Sok cares about is finally having the satisfaction of reading his last words printed at the end of his book: *Everyone's doomed!* His work's done. Sok's killed his beast. He's never been happier.

But the beast was captured, and with him the false prophet who had performed the miraculous signs on his behalf. With these signs he had deluded those who had received the mark of the beast and worshiped his image. The two of them were thrown alive into the fiery lake of burning sulfur.

REVELATION 19:20